Born shortly before the Second Wo
in a close and loving family in the
world of show business. His father
ing with top dance bands, including
during the 1920s and Geraldo in t
Binkie Stuart, popularly known as the British Shirley Temple. William himself had a brief career as a film star at the tender age of four, starring alongside Margaret Lockwood, Michael Wilding and Celia Johnson in the British comedy, *Dear Octopus*.

Throughout his life, William has taken the advice of his beloved Granny Fraser and worked hard towards achieving his heart's desire, whether that be buying his first car, running a luxurious hotel, or driving a Winnebago across Europe. However, it wasn't until he attended a training programme in the USA, hosted by guru Anthony Robbins, that he realised how much his mindset affected his outcomes. Realising that others remain as unaware as he once was of how the Law of Attraction influences their lives, William has made it his mission to share his experiences and knowledge through the pages of this book and the accompanying workshops.

William lives in Great Yarmouth with his wife Lucy, while his four children, now all in their thirties, live in various parts of the world. Although retired, he keeps himself busy playing an active role in running the workshops and giving practical demonstrations.

You can find out more about William's work or book yourself on one of his workshops.

www.theanswerunleashed.co.uk
sales@theanswerunleashed.co.uk

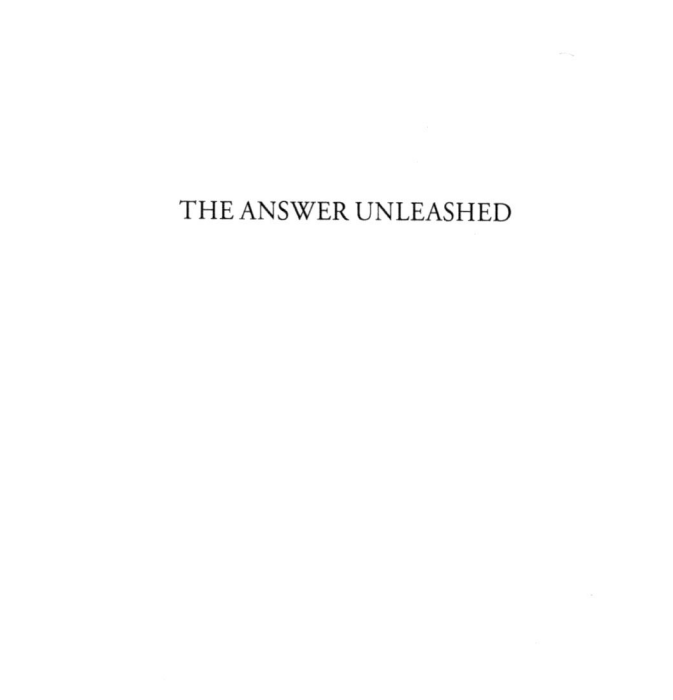

THE ANSWER UNLEASHED

THE ANSWER UNLEASHED

William Fraser

SilverWood

Published in 2018 by SilverWood Books

SilverWood Books Ltd
14 Small Street, Bristol, BS1 1DE, United Kingdom
www.silverwoodbooks.co.uk

Copyright © William Fraser 2018

The right of William Fraser to be identified as the author of this
work has been asserted in accordance with the Copyright, Designs and
Patents Act 1988 Sections 77 and 78.

All rights reserved. No part of this publication may be reproduced,
stored in a retrieval system, or transmitted in any form or by any means,
electronic, mechanical, photocopying, recording or otherwise,
without prior permission of the copyright holder.

ISBN 978-1-78132-804-0 (paperback)

British Library Cataloguing in Publication Data
A CIP catalogue record for this book is available from the British Library

Page design and typesetting by SilverWood Books

Printed on responsibly sourced paper

Contents

Acknowledgements	8
Introduction	10
Part I	14
Unexplained Events In My Early Life	16
The Power of Positivity	34
Growing Up and Moving On	56
Ragdale Hall	70
Good Things Come to Those Who Winnebago	92
Part II	104
Path to Positivity	106
The Law of Attraction	114
First Steps	122
Essential Tools and Techniques	134
Signposts	152
My Journey	170
Conclusion	176

Acknowledgements

I would like to thank Matt Coble for his help and support also my three daughters Emily Fraser, Francesca Fraser, Clementine Fraser and my son Julian Fraser whose encouragement made this book possible.

Introduction

As a child – and a gullible one, at that – I would believe most things I was told. Whatever happened to me, I would accept as normal. I thought miracles happened to everybody; I never questioned them.

For much of my life, I was not in control. I went with the flow, accepting whatever came my way. I thought I must simply be lucky – not that I ever relied on that luck. It just came to me whenever I needed it most.

I wouldn't say I was spiritual in my formative years, but the essence of a piece I read in a school textbook has stuck in my mind. It went something like this:

> The light shines brightest in a child.
> The light then goes out in adolescence.

> But only in old age does it return to shine,
> But never as bright as before.

My spiritual awareness returned to me later in life when I experienced a breakthrough in Miami. This was my turning point. Up until then, I had just been treading water, but life now had meaning. It was a transformation; my thinking changed completely. It was as if I could see the world through new eyes and recognise what I had been missing.

When I discovered the film *The Secret*, I knew that there was more to it than all the hype surrounding the movie and I decided to research further. I must admit, at first I found no results. Luckily, I persevered. At the back of my mind, it all made sense, and eventually, after a particularly interesting meditation session on the beach, I had a eureka moment. I had stumbled upon the missing formula; the pattern for living a full and contented life; the final piece of the giant jigsaw that is life and consciousness. It was so simple and so obvious, yet I had never caught a glimpse of it before.

The first part of this book is a collection of spiritual events, which I call my 'miracles', that have happened to me throughout my life. I am not a religious man; I have a spiritual awareness and faith in myself, both of which led me to delve deeper into the events that helped to shape my life. During my research and experiments, I found the Answer, and it is this I will share with you in Part II.

A miracle is powered by a force that we have no control over. It can come in the form of an opportunity or an unexpected event. I think miracles are commonplace – they can happen to anybody. Most people in the Western world go through life taking them for granted, not seeing them for what they are. When anything out of the ordinary happens to them, people will seek to rationalise it, relying too heavily on coincidence. A scientist will find a scientific explanation; a religious person will find a religious explanation; a spiritual person will find a spiritual explanation.

All the miracles that have come my way have been unforgettable, personal, and have strengthened my belief in cosmic forces.

Each one has been different. They have stayed with me throughout the years, and many have formed major events in my life. At these times, I have often wondered whether I have a guardian angel watching over me.

Simply put, miracles have made me who I am.

Part I

Everyday Miracles

Unexplained Events In My Early Life

Early childhood

I was born in August 1938. My mother's name was Florence Fraser, and she was an actress. My father, William Fraser, was a professional musician and played with the top dance bands of the time. He performed with Bert Ambrose & His Orchestra on a regular basis in the early 1920s at the prestigious Embassy Club in London, where many of the great British dance bands made their names.

The Embassy Club was part of a thriving entertainment industry between the First and Second World Wars. It earned a reputation for putting on great music, which lasted long into the post-war period. Some time after my father left Bert Ambrose & His Orchestra, Vera Lynn became their headline singer, taking them through the long war years. Meanwhile, my father joined Geraldo, one of the top bands of the 1930s.

It could be stressful being a part of a family which was geared towards producing one performance after another, but we stuck together through it. My father also worked hard as a chief inspector in an engineering factory, but he still found time to spend with my sister and me. Both he and my mother encouraged me to take up hobbies, including stamp collecting, model ship building, fishing and photography, which I still enjoy today.

In all, my early childhood was a cheerful, loving one.

The world at war

During the Second World War, everything was rationed and coupon books were worth more than money. Food was scarce and there were always long queues at the grocer's or the butcher's. People were encouraged to grow vegetables and keep chickens for their eggs, but often they went without goods we take for granted nowadays. Our family was very lucky; I don't ever remember a time when we went hungry.

My father built an air raid shelter at the bottom of the garden to keep us safe. It was half-submerged in the ground, with an earth mound over the top of it for extra insulation. When the warning siren went off, we had to stop whatever we were doing and scramble to safety.

Our air raid shelter was fitted out with two sets of wooden bunk beds. One of my earliest memories is of my father wrapping me in a blanket in the middle of the night and rushing me out to the safety of the shelter to continue my night's sleep in one of the bunks. We could feel the vibrations running through the earth when each bomb dropped.

On another occasion, the air raid siren went off during the day. My father was working, and I was at home with my mother and sister. There was not enough time between the first wails of the siren and the ominous sound of the Luftwaffe engines overhead for us to get down to the shelter, so we were forced to hide underneath the dining table. I can still remembering the three of us huddling together, the edges of the tablecloth brushing my mother's hair as she held us both as close as she could. I could hear my heart hammering in my chest – and I'm pretty sure I could hear my sister's and mother's hearts, too.

It was a terrifying experience. The enemy plane was directly above our street. Somehow, the pilot had managed to get under the barrage balloons, so he was flying very low. When he dropped a bomb, it felt like the whole house jumped off its foundations, shaking plaster dust from the ceiling and walls. There was an almighty thud on the back door, but none of us made a move. We were too afraid.

We waited for what seemed like an age for the all-clear to sound. When it finally did, we climbed out, stiff-limbed and shaken. A large piece of shrapnel was embedded in the back door, and we realised we were very lucky to be alive. Imagine what might have happened if we had tried to make it to the air-raid shelter – it doesn't bear thinking about.

During air raids, members of the Home Guard would man the rooftops of the town. They would sit out in the open on top of factories and municipal buildings, bravely returning fire with rickety machine guns that sounded like distant thunder. The Luftwaffe pilot who had nearly wiped us out was shot down soon after dropping his bomb on our street.

After the war, my father demolished the air raid shelter to build a pond, which played a big part in my childhood. I have many happy memories of fishing with a net in a nearby stream, catching an assortment of wildlife to inhabit our pond.

The British Shirley Temple

My sister, Alison, was seven years older than me, and we didn't have a great deal in common because of the age gap. She went to a theatrical school, and I remember going to pantomimes and plays to watch her perform. I was always very proud of my sister – she was a natural on the stage, as was our mother.

As a result of her own acting career, my mother had valuable and influential contacts in the film industry. She mentored my sister on the stage, and in 1936, at the tender age of four, Alison's dancing abilities saw her win her first film role, playing alongside George Formby in *Keep Your Seats Please*. Her character's name in the film was Binkie, and Alison adopted that as her stage name – Binkie Stuart. Known as the British Shirley Temple, she became something of a celebrity, going on to appear in a number of films over the course of 1937 and 1938, including *Little Miss Somebody*, *Rose of Tralee* and *Little Dolly Daydream*. Her finest cinematic moment was in 1938 when she starred alongside Maureen O'Hara in *My Irish Molly*.

Although the outbreak of the Second World War effectively ended Alison's film career, she went on to appear in shows with our parents, and the popularity of the British Shirley Temple lived on. I enjoyed the kudos that having a famous sister won me in the playground when I started school a few years later – everyone wanted to be friends with Binkie Stuart's brother.

Accidental audition

When I was four years old, my sister went for an audition at Ealing Studios for a part in the film, *Dear Octopus*. As my mother could not find a childminder that day, she had no choice but to take me along to the studios, too. I was told to be on my very best behaviour, but this instruction had little effect on my mischievous four-year-old mind.

Dear Octopus was a British comedy, directed by Harold French and starring Margaret Lockwood, Michael Wilding and Celia Johnson. Alison did not get the part. However, the casting director had been watching me playing, and he chose me instead.

I was cast in the part of Joe, a very naughty little boy, and let me tell you, this part suited me down to the ground. As I recall, the producer in particular had a hard time controlling me – I don't think he understood children very well. I would get tired and fed up with all the waiting around and having to do scenes over and over, and he would try everything to persuade me to play along. He would even bribe me with sweets and pocket money, but to no avail. I wasn't having any of it.

For example, in one of the scenes, I was supposed to walk past a bedroom door on the first floor, pulling a toy cart along behind me. The object was for Michael Wilding to open the bedroom door, trip over the toy cart and tumble down the stairs, and as I'm sure you can imagine, the timing had to be exactly right. If I walked too quickly or too slowly, he would miss the cart and the scene wouldn't work. It took a lot of practice and a great many takes to get the scene exactly right, but I'm afraid I was not particularly cooperative. Exasperated, the producer finally called my father in, and he made the whole thing into a game. This worked much better – suddenly it was fun again.

I wasn't really an actor, not in the way my sister was – I didn't have the same level of experience. Still, it was an exciting time; I had great fun on the film set and was spoiled rotten by the crew and actors. If you feel like seeing a small child trip Michael Wilding down the stairs, *Dear Octopus* is well worth a watch. I'm listed under my stage name: Alistair Stewart.

Bus trouble

In July 1945, two weeks before my seventh birthday, people were still elated from the end of the War and the festivities and parties in the streets to celebrate Victory in Europe (VE) Day. In the mornings, my mother would take me to school, but as she worked in the local factory in the afternoons, she was unable to pick me up at the end of the school day. Instead, I would have to catch the number 484 bus by myself.

Things were different in those days; parents didn't have the same concerns as they do now about letting their children go on the bus alone. But then again, I was only six years old. Without fail, my mother would make sure that she was waiting for me at the bus stop when I arrived home.

To this day, I still remember that my bus was a dark green double decker. In those days, the buses didn't have doors like they do now. People would step on a metal platform to get on to the bus, and hang on to a pole while waiting to get off. There were two different types of bus stop, then: an official bus stop, which had a big post in the ground or a bus shelter, and an unofficial stop where passengers simply stuck out their hands to indicate they wanted to get on. The buses always stopped at the official bus stops, but if no one was waiting at the unofficial ones, the driver would carry on without stopping. My stop was an official bus stop on a busy main road: the A4 London Road in Langley.

Every day when I knew I was getting close to home, I would walk up to the front of the bus and wait next to the driver until we reached my stop. And every day, as he was supposed to, the driver would stop the bus so that I could get off into the arms of my waiting mother. But on one particular scorching hot summer's day, the driver didn't stop the bus. He just carried on going at quite some speed. I have no idea why – maybe he was running late and trying to make up time.

I panicked. To a confused six-year-old, the driver not stopping the bus was extremely frightening. I didn't know where I would end up if I didn't get off the bus where my mother was waiting. Being so young, I didn't realise the speed at which the bus was travelling; all I knew was that I had to get off the bus immediately.

It's strange the things you remember clearly from events that happened a long time ago. The brief flash memories I have from that day are as vivid as if it were yesterday, and they will stay ingrained in my mind for ever. My mother was wearing a white dress with a floral pattern and white open-toed shoes. Her hair was tied back and she stood with her hands clasped in front of her, smiling as she saw me approaching on the bus. It may be that I remember this all so clearly because it is the last memory of that day before everything went black. I can still see her smile fading as she realised two things: the bus wasn't going to stop, and what I was about to do as a result. But it was all too late – I had already stepped off the bus.

I don't even remember my foot touching the ground.

My poor mother later said it was as though everything happened in slow motion. I was catapulted off the bus like a rag doll being thrown around, hit a lamp post and bounced off a garden wall before coming to rest next to the road on a grass verge in front of a row of houses. Everyone who saw it happen thought I must be dead. My mother thought I was dead. There was no way a small boy could possibly have survived that.

In the immediate aftermath of the accident, as I recall, I was looking down as though I was floating above my body. I was wearing grey shorts and a light blue short-sleeved shirt, which was all ripped and covered in dirt and blood, and I thought, *My mum's going to be so cross, my shirt is all muddy.* I didn't think anything of this memory when I was a young boy, but having discussed it with people in later years, I've come to realise that I experienced an out-of-body experience. It was very quick, just a flash of a memory, but I'm sure that's what I experienced.

An ambulance picked me up and took me to the hospital. When the doctors saw the state I was in, they weren't hopeful. They told my parents that it was remarkably lucky that I hadn't been killed instantly, and that they would do their best under the circumstances.

I had a fractured skull, and was black and blue from head to toe, with cuts all over my face and body. My mother said I was completely unrecognisable; my face was so swollen that I looked nothing like the son she knew and loved so much. I was wired up to drips and tubes and was in a deep coma. The doctors estimated that there was only a 5% chance of me ever waking up and advised my parents to prepare for the worst, but my mother and father prayed every day and, like most parents in their situation, never gave up hope.

Amazingly, I proved the doctors wrong. Three weeks later, I opened my eyes, shocking the doctors who had been so sure that this little boy would never wake up. Even my parents admitted to being somewhat surprised, after the depressing forewarnings they had received.

When I woke up, I couldn't speak and felt confused and disorientated. I remember drifting in and out of consciousness for a while and my mother constantly being by my bedside. My parents were naturally thrilled and relieved that I had woken up, but I was still very weak. Three weeks in a coma is a long time for a seven-year-old (unluckily for me, I had slept through my birthday) and it took me a while before I was strong enough to start walking again.

The drips were removed and the doctors would allow me to take small sips of orange squash, but only a little bit at a time. I remember on one occasion waking up feeling so unbelievably thirsty that my tongue was stuck to the roof of my mouth. Then I noticed the orange squash on my bedside table and drank the whole lot. After that, I started to get better.

Once the doctors were sure I was going to survive, I was transferred to a convalescent home to regain my strength and rehabilitate before going home. The convalescent home was for injured soldiers who had returned from the War, and some had limbs missing or were in wheelchairs. I was the only child on the ward; it was a very unusual situation.

The soldiers wore blue suits, white shirts and red ties, which was the uniform for those who had returned from the War injured. I remember thinking that they were very brave and looked so smart in their uniforms. They took me under their wings; when my parents had left after their daily visits, the soldiers would come and keep me company, involving me in their card games or showing me magic tricks.

Some weeks later, I had more energy and my injuries were healing well, so I was allowed to go home. The soldiers stood (or sat in their wheelchairs) outside the main entrance of the convalescent home and waved to me as my father pulled out of the driveway. It was sad to say goodbye to these brave men who had become my friends, but I was happy to be going back to my family. I was well on my way to recovery, but it would still be a few more weeks before I was able to leave the house and go back to school.

I never took the bus again. After the accident, my mother always collected me from school. It was about half an hour's walk through Green Drive, a beautiful wooded track with overhanging willow trees casting most of the road in shadow, and no cars were allowed. We were both grateful to have this time together after I had so nearly lost my life.

My mother would tell me all sorts of stories on the way to and from school. Most of the stories were about the animals we saw as we walked, or poems she had read or learned in her childhood. I don't remember many of them now, but one that comes to mind is a poem she made up one day when we saw a rabbit:

> One fine morn in early spring,
> When Saint Mary's bells went ding-a-ling,
> A little brown bunny went scampering by
> And before I could wink the other eye,
> Along came a jolly old sandy hare,
> So then I just stood and watched the pair.
> And then from yonder chestnut tree
> A blackbird chirped his song of glee.
> Blackbird, hare and little brown bunny
> Made that beautiful spring morning
> So joyous and funny.

It's strange what sticks with you. St Marys, as it happens, is where my mother is buried. I think of her – and that little brown bunny – often.

Summer camp on the Isle of Wight

In 1949, my school took part in a big camping trip involving boys from lots of other schools. Only six boys from each school were chosen to go, and I was lucky enough to be one of the few. I was eleven years old at the time and tremendously excited, as this was the first time I had ever been away from home on my own.

We had been given a list of essential items to take with us, and one of the items on the list was a jackknife. As I didn't have one, I asked around friends and family to see if I might borrow one. Under instruction from our father, my older sister reluctantly lent me her jackknife, stressing that I must take great care of it and bring it back in the same condition as it had been when she lent it to me.

The six boys chosen to go on the trip were to meet in the

morning at our school in Langley, Buckinghamshire, and then travel by coach to Portsmouth to catch a ferry to the Isle of Wight. I had never been on a boat, and the night before I left for camp, I couldn't sleep for excitement.

However, as I walked eagerly up to the school gates the following morning, the enthusiasm began to seep out of my body as I recognised one of the other boys waiting for the coach. The school bully was standing among the group. Whenever there was trouble at school, he was at the centre of it. Although he was in my class and only a few months older than me, he was much bigger, and he was well known in the local area for his cruel and menacing behaviour. Like most bullies, he had his little gang of followers who pretended to like him and did as he told them so that they wouldn't become his next victims. Basically, everyone was scared of him.

Frowning slightly, I slowed down as I approached the school gates, deciding to adopt my usual defence tactic when it came to the bully – I would keep my head down and avoid him as best I could. Usually this worked, but that was when we were in a class of thirty pupils where my presence was easily lost among my peers. In a small group of six boys, I knew it wouldn't be quite so simple, but I had been looking forward to this trip for so long. Innocently optimistic, I was determined to enjoy myself regardless.

En-route to Portsmouth to catch the ferry, we stopped off at a transport café called the Dolly Varden. As the six of us sat outside on stools at a rickety old wooden table and drank hot chocolate, the bully was boasting about stealing a slingshot from a small boy who lived on his street. The boy's father had hand carved it for his birthday, and the bully found it highly amusing that after he'd stolen the slingshot, the boy had run away crying. I wasn't sure if it was my paranoia or not, but it seemed that while the bully was telling his story, he was looking at me more than the other boys. Ever the optimist, I decided that as he seemed to be including me in his group, maybe the camping trip wouldn't be so bad after all. Maybe he would leave me alone.

Finally we reached the Isle of Wight. The campsite was in a huge field not far from the beach, with a large marquee where we would eat our meals and several smaller ridge tents, each sleeping six people. Unfortunately for me, the school bully was one of the boys sleeping in my tent.

We soon knuckled down to a regimented way of life, an army camp for eleven-year-olds, waking up at seven o'clock and laying out our kit for inspection once we were washed and dressed. Every day, we would take part in group activities, which included a tour of the island and a visit to Carisbrooke Castle. We also had a portion of the day free to write letters, read or play.

One day during our free time, I was on the beach playing in the rock pools. Nearby, the bully was with a group of boys from other schools. Instead of hitting a ball, he was using a rounders bat to launch live crabs. A man walking his dog on the beach reported the bully's cruel behaviour to a camp teacher, but when the teacher spoke to the bully, he lied and said that the crabs had already been dead. This was typical of the bully: he was sneaky as well as cruel.

Then came the morning when the bully inevitably singled me out for attention. As we lay our kit out on our beds ready for inspection, my jackknife, borrowed from my sister, was on display. My heart sank as the bully sauntered over to my bed, a nasty smile on his face.

"I like your knife," he said, "and I haven't got one. Tell you what, I'll 'borrow' yours."

I wasn't foolish enough to argue with him, so I just stayed quiet and hoped that I'd get the knife back in one piece.

At lunchtime, the bully came up to the table I was sitting at. Laughing, he told me that he had hidden my knife and I would never find it. I was devastated by this news. I was missing my mum and dad; I was alone and insecure; I had placed a lot of importance on my sister's jackknife, and now it was lost. In 1949, only a few years after the war had ended, people didn't have a lot of money to buy new things, so my parents had taught me to respect other people's property. That was the worst thing of all – I felt that I had let my family down.

Feeling tearful, I found solitude in a nearby wood where I could let my emotions run freely – I didn't want the other boys to see me crying.

Knowing my sister would be furious if I returned home without her knife, I had to find it, but it could have been hidden anywhere. Was it far away from where I was standing, or was it buried within a few feet of me? The task ahead of me was massive. If it had not been for my belief system at the time – some may call it the innocence of childhood – I would have given up there and then. Instead, thinking that anything was possible, I set out to find my sister's knife.

Walking for about half a mile in one direction chosen at random, I found myself on a wide sandy beach. I sat down to rest and ponder the next step in my mission, and completely lost track of time. When I had arrived on the beach, the tide had been in, and the next thing I knew, it was going out again. As more and more of the beach was revealed, enormous rocks started to appear. They stood along the entire stretch of sand, making the beach look almost otherworldly.

As I noticed these huge rocks appearing, for reasons I am still unable to explain, I felt total calmness spreading within me. Before long, the anxiety that had plagued me all afternoon had disappeared. Despite being completely alone on this eerie-looking beach, I wasn't afraid. Perhaps my calm was simply a result of being in the presence of the ocean, so vast and immense, which is something that still affects me today. It is easy to feel insignificant when I'm looking out to sea, limitless water stretching before my eyes, which is a peaceful and humbling experience and helps to put life's problems in perspective. Even as a young boy, I remember feeling this sense of insignificance.

Or perhaps it was a higher power at work.

As I studied the rocks, I noticed that they were all covered in slimy seaweed. Without thinking about what I was doing, I stood up and walked slowly along the beach in between the rocks, which, if I recall correctly, were almost my height, kicking up wet sand as I went. A little crab climbed out of a pool of water at the base of one of the rocks and I stopped to watch it. The crab slowly made its way along the sand, and I followed.

After a short while, I found myself standing in front of another rock. There was nothing unusual about this rock; it looked just the same as all the others: big and covered in slimy seaweed. I lost sight of the crab, or perhaps I just lost interest in following it. At this point, I don't think I was conscious of what I was doing. Reaching out, I lifted up a clump of seaweed that was hanging on the rock – the big rock that looked like all the other big rocks on the beach – and can you guess what was underneath?

I truly could not believe my eyes. There, right in front of me, was my sister's jackknife. The power of my thoughts and my desire had drawn me to that exact location, leading me to the knife that I so desperately wanted to find. It really was astonishing and the memory of it has stayed with me throughout my life and reinforced both my faith and my belief system. To this day, just thinking about it makes the hairs on the back of my neck stand on end. Should doubt ever creep into my belief system, I cast my mind back to that day and my faith is restored.

As an adult, I can look back and recognise that the power of my mind and the universe worked together to lead me to the knife. This was the Law of Attraction at work. If that happened without me even being conscious of what I was doing, imagine the power *you* can have if you really put your mind to it. Surely, anything is possible.

Learning to rise above
The bullying at Langley Secondary School grew steadily worse, and I was one of the bullies' favourite victims. After a while, my parents couldn't help but notice a change in my personality – I became sullen and withdrawn, and I started coming up with excuses not to go to school. If I couldn't avoid school, I would try to hide in the playground so as not to get picked on.

Two boys in particular were horrendously unpleasant – and not just to me. I would avoid them like the plague, and even now, when

I look back, I regard them as evil. They were out of control – not even the teachers could rein them in. On one occasion, when one of the teachers tried to intercede on behalf of a bullied student, these two reprobates beat him up instead.

Unsurprisingly, the bullying began to have a negative impact on my health and my schoolwork. When my parents found out what was happening to me, they were horrified, and to my intense relief, they moved me to another school. I had such faith in my parents and I knew they would come up with the right solution; I only wished I had told them about the bullying before it started having a lasting effect on me.

Before I started at the new school, my father sat me down and told me that he could not fight my battles for me. I had to stand on my own two feet, and to this end, he decided to teach me how to fight properly – even dirtily, if I had to. Over the next few weeks, my father trained with me every day. There were no Queensbury Rules, just simple self-defence and the psychological means to overcome my fears. Of course, that was easier said than done. Even as a kid, I knew it would be me facing up to the bullies, and they had terrified me for years.

My father taught me four simple lessons:

- Lesson one – take the bully by surprise.
- Lesson two – get in the first blow and aim for their weakest point if you can, e.g. their shins. The trick is to weaken the bully without leaving yourself open to attack.
- "Imagine his shins are a football," my father would tell me. "And you're going to score the goal of the season."
- With this in mind, my father bought me some boots to wear at school, instead of the soft shoes I had been wearing. Those boots made me feel safe.
- Lesson three – after the first kick, the bully will automatically stoop to where the pain is. This is instinct; he won't be able to help himself. When he does, raise your right kneecap up to catch his chin with as much force as you can muster.

Of course, you will feel the pain of this move, too, but that's the thing about violence: it can hurt the person dealing it out as much as the person receiving it.
- Now the bully is in a vulnerable position, completely at your mercy.
- Lesson four – always be ready to run in case the plan doesn't work.

Every day before school and every evening afterwards, I would practise the art of self-defence. Over time, I could feel myself growing stronger and faster, and with that I began to gain confidence.

Seeing the positive changes in me, my father told me that I must take care not to become a bully myself, because mindless violence can result in serious trouble. I must only use my fighting skill in self-defence, or to protect someone else. I assured him that a bully was something I would never be – it went against every part of my character.

My father also taught me that I would be an unknown quantity at my new school. There would be bullies, and they would test me in order to see where I ought to be in the social pecking order. He told me not to show any fear, because fear is irresistible to a bully. They are exceptionally good at recognising it in others, and they seek it out primarily because they themselves are afraid. This is why they never pick on anyone they perceive to be bigger or stronger than they are.

The fateful day finally came – the first day of term at my new school, the Orchard Secondary School in Slough. I must admit that I was pretty nervous, but I settled in quite quickly. Having been a victim of bullies at my previous school, I could pick out exactly who the predators were in my new environment, and I kept an eye on them, as watchful as a meerkat.

There was one particular boy who didn't like to fight people himself – possibly because he didn't want to get into trouble, or get hurt. Instead, he would force two smaller kids to fight, pretending to act as referee while they went for each other. He seemed to take enjoyment from watching them hurt each other. A particularly nasty specimen, he would kick any reluctant combatant mercilessly until they agreed to fight. It was unpleasant to watch.

In my first term at the school, I made a few good friends and was beginning to enjoy my time there. My schoolwork improved and I was no longer nervous and withdrawn all the time. I managed to avoid this troublemaker for a whole term, which was pretty impressive. The Orchard wasn't a particularly large school, but perhaps it took him a long time to tire of his usual victims. I continued to train with my father every day before and after school and throughout the holiday, and my uniform boots felt like a shield.

I was ready for the new term to begin.

The bully was up to his usual tricks as soon as the first bell went. It seemed he had run out of victims, because he came looking for fresh meat to feed his perverted desire for violence. Before long, his sights were set on me, and the dreaded day where I would have to stand up for myself had arrived.

As he picked on one of my friends and me, demanding that we fight each other while he 'refereed', I felt very frightened. I had never been in a real fight before – when the bullies at the old school had attacked me, it had always been rather one-sided – and I don't like violence. It went against my nature to inflict pain on another person, especially one of my friends. I was badly out of my comfort zone.

It was time to put into practice the lessons my father had spent so long teaching me, but with the fear welling up inside me and the adrenaline pumping through my veins, that was easier said than done. Fleetingly, I considered lesson four – running – but decided against it. There was already a ring of students around us, and any attempt to escape would have been blocked – not to mention the trouble it would have set me up for in the long run. I would have been marked out as a coward: fair game for anyone in the playground. I began to wish that my father had been able to give me the courage I so badly needed along with the fighting skills, but he was right – I couldn't rely on him. I had to fight my own battles – and I was no coward.

Something inside me snapped and the fear spilled over into

anger, which clouded my mind. All I knew was that I had to stop this in a way that meant neither my friend nor I would be hurt. As the bully gave his order for the fight to begin, I lost my temper and shouted at him that I wouldn't fight my friend. I would fight him, the bully, instead.

In some ways, I had already ignored lesson one: take the bully by surprise. But it had been a long time since anyone had stood up to this bully, so in that respect, it was an unexpected turn of events for him, and it worked well enough. When he found a smaller, much angrier boy bearing down on him, he didn't even have time to raise his fists.

I screamed at him, the rage burning inside me. I did not visualise a football, as my father had taught me; I simply went straight for his bony shins, bare and unprotected by his school shorts. There was an almighty crack as my boot made contact, and a shriek as he dropped like a stone. I was very lucky to have hit my target, thinking back – I suspect things would have gone badly for me if I had missed. With all my weeks of training behind me, my knee was ready and waiting for his chin. He went down like a sack of potatoes.

At that stage, I am ashamed to say, I lost all semblance of control. I had him on the ground, and with the rage boiling inside me, I laid into him, punching his nose and face over and over again. The crowd around us had grown quite large, filled with spectators astonished at the turn of events. This was a different fight to the usual playground scrap. It was quite a thing to witness one of the worst school bullies getting a taste of his own medicine.

Eventually, someone must have gone to fetch the prefects, because the next thing I knew, I was being dragged off the crying boy on the ground and frog-marched to the headmaster's office. I was punished, of course. It was corporal punishment in those days, and despite the fact that corporal punishment is completely immoral, given the way I had hurt the bully, I deserved it. My sense of achievement blotted out the pain of the cane.

The incident on the playground did not go unnoticed. I had simply defended my friend, and myself, so I was quite surprised by the older kids' reaction. I was branded a hero, and everybody wanted to be my friend – including the other bullies. Even the teachers were aware of what had happened. I believe all the staff at the school had known exactly what the bully was doing, forcing other kids to fight, but they had chosen to turn a blind eye to it, chalking it up to 'boys being boys' – whatever that means. Deep down, I suspect the teachers and prefects were all rather relieved to see this particular low-life taken down a peg or two.

Looking back now, I can see that I had done the unthinkable: risen above the bullies. From that day onwards, I was elevated to a level where I would never have to fight to defend myself again throughout my entire school career.

The Power of Positivity

My first job after leaving school was as a junior salesman. I used to cycle to work, this being my only form of transport, but as a sixteen-year-old dreamer, what I really wanted was a car. A couple of my peers thought that stealing cars was the way forward, but fortunately I chose a different route.

The redoubtable Granny Fraser

My grandmother had led a hard life. A shrewd and strong-willed lady, she brought up three sons in Glasgow during the Victorian age with not much money to spare. Whatever Granny Fraser put her mind to, she succeeded at.

She was proud of her achievements and often demonstrated how fit and healthy she was. Even when she was well into her nineties, she was still able to touch her toes without bending her knees.

I thought she ought to have been a dancer, given how physically fit she was. She did not act like an old lady. Tall, erect and dignified, she was a woman to be taken seriously. She would tell everyone she met that she was going to live to be one hundred years old. In the end, she didn't quite achieve her final goal, passing away at the ripe old age of ninety-seven.

A great lady, sadly missed.

Her main aim in life was to educate her three children, my father being the eldest, and give them the best possible start in life. She guided my father and my uncle Jimmy to study music. At the time, there was a great call for talented musicians, and she recognised the fact that they could have successful careers if they played well enough. I remain convinced to this day that she was the driving force behind my father's success in the music business.

After my grandfather died in the late 1950s, Granny Fraser moved south to come and live with us. She was a great help to me, teaching me things about life that I never learned at school and helping to guide me on to the right path in life. She had been a Lecturer in Psychology when she was younger, and she taught me that nothing is impossible if you set your mind to it. This lesson has stayed with me to this day.

I loved her dearly and couldn't have asked for a better mentor. If she was still alive today, how different my life might have been.

The car – my pride and joy

In 1953, my class went on a school trip to the Ford factory in Dagenham. The car of the moment was the Ford Zephyr Mark 1, and at the time, I imagined owning one of these beautiful cars. Obsessed with cars, I would go to the Earls Court Motor Show every year with my father, an event I was always very excited about. I longed to have a car of my own, but given my limited means at the time, I believed it was an impossible dream.

One day, Granny Fraser suggested to me that I should save money by coming home for lunch. This seemed like a good idea, so I worked out the logistics of getting home and back to work in time, and put the plan into action. Every day, along with my lunch, I would have a twenty-minute lecture from my grandmother. At first I didn't take what she was telling me seriously, but after a while, it dawned on me that her advice made a lot of sense. After all, what did I have to lose?

When I told Granny Fraser that I wanted a new car, she told me the first step towards getting one was to go to the local showroom and pick up a brochure for the car of my choice.

"Here's the brochure, Gran," I said jokingly, presenting it to her the next day, "so where's my new car?"

Of course, she told me it wasn't as easy as that – I would have to follow her process. We opened the brochure and found a large poster of the car I really wanted. She told me to put it up on my bedroom wall – the car would be the first thing I would see in the morning and the last thing I would see at night. Then, she told me that I would start to notice the car everywhere I went, and every time I saw it, it would reinforce the image in my mind.

Today, this is what I know as the Law of Attraction, but I had no knowledge of it in the 1950s.

The next part of Granny Fraser's process was her list of six financial rules. My grandmother told me that any fool could spend money, but it took a wise man to save it. It sounds such a simple thing to say, but there is a knack to saving. Of course, very few of us are blessed with the means to purchase a home outright, so mortgages are a necessity, but Granny Fraser impressed on me the importance of avoiding any other debts. Many people don't understand the power of money, and this is one of the reasons that debt is such an enormous problem in the modern world – the banks have the money and people pay *them* interest to borrow it. This is entirely the wrong way around.

If only everyone followed my grandmother's rules:

- Rule one – you work hard to earn your money, so don't throw it away on trivial things. Ask yourself, "Do I really need this?"

- Rule two – learn the value of money.
- Rule three – budget your wages.
- Rule four – save on a regular basis, even if you don't think you can afford it. Remember, the things that seem so important today are the rubbish of the future.
- Rule five – make sacrifices. What are you regularly spending money on that you could do without?
- Rule six – watch your savings grow and enjoy the power of your money.

If you follow the rules of money, you will become wealthy. Money makes money, so if you can, only ever spend the interest your savings earn.

Once Granny Fraser had helped me work out all my finances, she suggested that I get a part-time job to increase the amount I could save. I approached the owner of the local corner shop, Monty, for whom I had previously worked as an errand boy, delivering orders on the trade bike, and he was happy to take me on again. My part-time job involved stacking shelves and cleaning up the shop for three hours a night on top of my full-time job as a junior salesman. I also worked in the shop on Wednesday afternoons and Sundays, which boosted my earnings considerably.

In some ways, I grew up in that shop, having worked for Monty on and off since I was fourteen. In fact, I often found myself spending more time with Monty and his wife than at home with my family. Monty's wife was a marvellous cook and always invited me to share Sunday roast with them, which I looked forward to all week. That was typical of their generosity, although I think Monty and his wife enjoyed my company as much as I enjoyed their food and hospitality. Monty and I would play chess in the drawing room after lunch, and I usually ended up staying for Sunday tea. Certainly in terms of food, Sunday was the highlight of the week for my teenage self.

Thanks to my part-time earnings, my savings grew more rapidly than before. When I had saved up £100, my grandmother advised me to go window-shopping to remind myself why I was saving and reinforce the power of my money. I would do the same when I had £200, and so on. It was a very effective technique – I was fast becoming obsessed with saving every penny I could.

I always seemed to window shop for the things I could not afford, perhaps as a means to curb any temptation to part with my hard-earned cash too quickly. All sorts of things made up my 'window shopping', including glossy magazines like *Country Life* where I was drawn to the property section. I was passionate about period property and often fantasised about what life was like in old houses in the past. My peers and work colleagues would accuse me of having delusions of grandeur, but little did they know, these weren't delusions; they were predictions. I was determined to make my dreams happen; it was only a matter of time. With Granny Fraser's excellent advice and wisdom, anything was possible.

Within a few years, after I had passed my driving test, I got a new job as a sales demonstrator, which involved driving the company van. In those days, customers would part-exchange their old television sets, stereograms and so on, and the salesman who had made the sale was entitled to first refusal on the part-exchanged items. I capitalised on this opportunity and bought most of the exchanged stock, which I would clean, mend and sell on for a profit. In fact, I did so well at this that I started holding a monthly house-clearance sale.

I remember the day I went into the car showroom to order my dream car. All the salesmen knew me by then as I was always there, admiring my car-to-be. By the time I was able to purchase my first car, it was no longer the Ford Zephyr that was the top of the range – I bought a Ford Zodiac Mark II. It was two-tone – maroon and grey – with white wall tyres and chrome trim. Superb!

In those days, to own a new car was to stand out from the crowd. It was a rare occurrence for anyone to purchase a brand-new top-of-the-range car for cash, so there was a great deal of prestige in it. I was tremendously proud of my new car – and of the hard work that had earned it. I would clean the car daily, and it was still as good as new when I sold it on five years later to fund the deposit for my first self-employment venture.

Good things come to those who...

Needless to say, my new car didn't go unnoticed by my work colleagues. It was obvious that I could not afford a car like this on my wages, so several of them thought my father must have given it to me. The store manager even said to me that I must be on the fiddle! I didn't enlighten them, instead letting them think what they wanted. After all, it was really none of their business.

Around this time, I arranged a trip down to Brighton with my friends. We planned to take two car loads, with twelve people going in total, but unfortunately, my friend Jeff – the other car driver – had been to a wedding the day before the trip and was suffering from a merciless hangover. He had to pull out, leaving us one driver short.

Faced with a dilemma, I decided to borrow the company van, for which I had the keys, in order to fit everyone in one vehicle – not the best idea I have ever had! With twelve people on board, the balance was unsteady and the van was swerving all over the road. It wasn't long before I was stopped by the police and arrested for dangerous driving. To make matters worse, I wasn't insured to drive it on a Sunday – the van was only insured for business use. When the police had to get in touch with the company to check this, I was in *real* trouble.

My friends thought it was a proper lark to be pulled over by the police and continued to enjoy themselves, until they were also arrested. On the journey to Hendon Police Station, the humour subsided pretty dramatically. Now that they recognised the severity of the situation, my friends became much more supportive and tried to share the blame.

When the police finally released us, we returned home with our tails between our legs. I spent a sleepless night, going over and over the potential ramifications of my actions in my mind. Would I be fired? What would I do for work? Where could I go? Who would employ me with the criminal record I was bound to end up with? I was panicking, convinced that this one mistake would force my life down a bad path. Had I completely ruined my future?

When I got to work, it seemed that my worst fears were about to be confirmed. The manager told me not to start work; instead, I had to wait until the bosses from head office arrived. At this stage, I just knew I was going to be sacked.

However, I was wrong. After giving me a good telling off, to my amazement, the bosses promoted me to manage one of the smallest shops in the company. It felt entirely unreal to me in the moment, but as I live and breathe, this really happened. In fact, over the next four years, I was promoted another three times, ending up managing the largest store in the company.

It was a mystery that was to remain unsolved until I finally came to leave the company. When I handed in my notice, the managing director came to see me, trying to persuade me to stay. He offered to promote me to Southern Regional Area Manager, a role that would bring with it a handsome pay rise, but I refused.

Crestfallen, he then told me that he'd suspected all along I would eventually go to work for my father. For a moment, I was confused, as I had no wish to work in the engineering factory with my dad.

Then everything – the promotions; the fact that I wasn't sacked for my misadventures with the van – became clear as the MD carried on talking. My work colleagues had all thought I was the son of Hugh Fraser! Things made a lot more sense now I knew about these rumours – which had all started with my purchase of a brand new Ford Zodiac. In a way, that car – and my gran – had ensured my promotion for years.

Three days of Hell in Liverpool

I have always been interested in motor racing, both in terms of motorbikes and cars. At school, having to choose a sporting event on which to base a composition, I chose to write about the twenty-four hour Le Mans race that takes place every year in France.

As soon as I was old enough, I bought my first motorbike. At the age of sixteen, I was the proud owner of a BSA 250 C10L side valve – my pride and joy. At the time, my gran asked me whether this purchase was a wise move as it deviated from my plan of saving money for a car, but I told her I was intending to trade the motorbike in when I bought my car, gaining useful experience and road sense in the meantime.

The freedom of the open road and the sense of adventure that came from riding my bike were amazing. I joined a motorcycle club and would go for a ride most Sundays with my fellow bikers. We even went to the Isle of Man TT Races two years in a row (1957 and 1958).

Even when my motorcycling days were over, I still loved going back to the Isle of Man for the TT Races, held every year during the first week of June. It's a gregarious event, an opportunity to meet up with old friends and either compete against them or watch them racing around the island's roads. Of course, the races are not without their dangers, and riders are often killed, but the thrill is what keeps people coming back.

The highlight of the week's events is always the Senior TT race 500cc: the final race held on the Friday. To my annoyance, when I attended in 1958, the Senior TT race had to be postponed to the following day due to poor weather conditions (always a risk in the middle of the Irish Sea). Before going to the island, like any seasoned traveller, I had booked my transport home to save money and complication. Now, however, if I stayed to watch my favourite race, I stood a good chance of missing the ferry back to the mainland, which would connect with my coach home. The coach was unusually reliable and always left on time.

I decided to take the risk and watch the race, a decision which resulted in a mad dash to the ferry terminal at the far end of Douglas. I arrived, hot and flustered, only to see the ferry sailing off into the distance – I had missed it by a matter of minutes.

Cursing my luck, I waited for the next ferry, which wasn't due to leave for several hours. It was a complete disaster. I had carefully budgeted the money I had taken with me to last me through the week, right up to the last day – but I had not taken any change of plans into consideration. Feeling foolish and vulnerable – and I did not like that feeling one bit – I lamented my lack of foresight. I could easily have budgeted for an emergency, or decided not to tempt fate by watching the final race. The problems I faced were all of my own making and I was entirely responsible for the events of the coming days.

When I stepped off the ferry terminal in Liverpool, I was lost, alone and stranded in an unfamiliar city with no money. The next coach wasn't going to come for several days – and in any case, my ticket had only been valid for one particular journey. It was unlikely that the conductor would let me on without a replacement. All I had were the clothes I stood up in and my holiday suitcase full of dirty washing.

First things first: I had to look for a place to sleep for the long, chilly night ahead. Although I didn't know why at the time, I had always managed to land on my feet before, because I had always responded to the cosmic forces of the Universe. Now, though, I had created a situation in which they could not help me, and my good luck in life to date had not equipped me with any survival techniques.

Distraught, I decided to try to sleep on one of the hard benches in the waiting area of the ferry terminal. Although it was the first week of June, no one seemed to have informed the weather that spring had come to an end, and the nights were very cold. I didn't even have any winter clothing with me, since the days of the races had been forecast to be warm. For hours, I drifted in and out of consciousness, shivering with cold and watching the clock on the wall. As is often the case in times of misery, time seemed to stretch out to eternity. Every minute felt like an hour, and every hour seemed like a day.

Fortunately, I was alone in the ferry terminal, so I was able to change into extra clothing – not something I would attempt in today's world of constant monitoring and CCTV. I put on double layers of underwear and shirts. The extra clothes might not have been clean, but they did help to keep out the cold.

After a long, uncomfortable night without any real sleep, I came to as the hustle and bustle of the day in the port began in earnest. The ferry staff arrived along with the cleaners and caterers, all busily preparing the building for the day ahead. It was time to move on.

I didn't know Liverpool – I was a stranger here, but as most British cities follow the same sort of organisational logic, I was able to use this fact to my advantage. I found a public convenience where I could have a wash and brush up. After a long drink of water, feeling much cleaner, I set out towards what I imagined to be the town centre where it was likely I would find food outlets. By this point I was weak with hunger, having last eaten on the Isle of Man. My only possession was my suitcase, which seemed to grow heavier with every step I took.

Life is almost impossible to navigate in Western society when you have no money in your pocket. At each café, I told my story of woe, offering my services for an hour in exchange for food and drink, but most places turned me away. Finally, when I felt I was about to expire from lack of food, I encountered a friendly assistant in one of the cafés who took pity on me. Telling me she had a son about my age, she went into the kitchen to see what she could find and brought out a sandwich that was left over from the day before. It couldn't be sold and had been destined for the bin, but I was tremendously grateful to accept it. She also brought me a cup of hot tea – she was an angel in a tabard. I was so grateful for this small gift – it must have meant so little to her, but at that moment, in my time of need, it meant the world to me.

Even though it was old and stale, the sandwich tasted impossibly delicious and I savoured every single bite. I can still taste it now. Mindful of my predicament, I ate half of it and wrapped the other half in a napkin to save for later. I didn't know when, or even if I would find more food.

My next priority was to try to find a place to keep warm overnight. I had arrived in Liverpool on a Saturday night, but now it was Sunday and everything was closed. The banks and businesses were all shut so people could attend church. Now I had to exist until Monday morning when the coach station would open again and I could begin my journey back home.

As I walked aimlessly through the unfamiliar streets of the Sunday-quiet city, I could hear church bells ringing and the distant sound of a choir. Briefly, I considered seeking refuge in one of the edifices of stone and faith, but I decided against it. What right had I to use God's house for my own selfish ends?

In the end, I gave up on my search for sanctuary and headed for a nearby park. The sun was out, so I decided to make the most of its heat while I could. I found an empty park bench and settled there for the rest of the day.

While I waited, counting the passing minutes, all I could think about was the second half of the sandwich the kind woman in the café had given me that morning, but I had to put off eating it for as long as I could. Sitting on that hard park bench, anticipating another night of shivering in the cold, I recalled my mother's words with a touch of irony:

"If you don't wrap up warm, you will catch your death of cold."

Those cold nights in Liverpool taught me a valuable lesson: never take things for granted. Since then I have fully appreciated what I have, no matter how small or insignificant it may appear to be. I know from experience that there is always someone in the world worse off – somewhere in the city, there was probably another lost soul in exactly the same predicament as me, but without the comfort of half a stale sandwich.

As my gran would say, "Count your blessings and always look on the bright side."

As I whiled away the time on the park bench, my attention was drawn to the shrubbery across the path. Ordinarily, my mind busy with the tasks and worries of everyday life, I would never have noticed such a small detail, but on that day, boredom had set in and I had nothing else to focus on. In the bushes, I could see what looked like a foil milk top, but there was something about it that didn't look right.

Upon further inspection, it turned out to be two shillings and sixpence. In today's money, it would have been worth about £1, but then I felt like I had struck gold.

My first thought was to use my treasure to buy a meal, but it was still Sunday and all the cafés had closed. I would have to make do with the other half of the stale sandwich, which by this point had become rock hard. It took some eating, but the effort it took to chew it made it last longer. My stomach had shrunk and the few mouthfuls of bread and indeterminate filling managed to fill the gap.

When the night came, I abandoned the park. It was too exposed on my bench, and the wind was adding an extra bite to the cold weather. Huddled in the lee of a shop doorway covered by a long display window, I spent my second uncomfortable night. Although I could sit on my suitcase instead of the ground, it made for a lumpy and uncomfortable mattress, and I quickly resigned myself to insomnia.

Stop, Thief!

Early in the morning, I was moved on by a policeman. He was sympathetic, but told me I couldn't sleep in a doorway, so I had no choice but to resume walking the streets.

I picked a direction and started walking with no real idea of where I was going. Wandering aimlessly, I heard the sound of a milk float behind me. Hungry and desperate, I was gripped by the compulsion to steal a bottle of milk – something I would ordinarily never have considered. I followed the milk float to a street of terraced houses where the front doors opened directly on to the pavement. Here, the milkman started leaving the bottles outside his customers' doors, and initially, I considered pinching a bottle directly from the float. I quickly realised it was too risky, though; the milkman was staying close to the float, probably to prevent kids from doing exactly what I was thinking about doing.

I let him finish his work and move on, waiting around the corner until the coast was clear. When the opportunity arose, I had to act fast – I wouldn't get too many chances now that the neighbourhood was beginning to wake up. Leaving my suitcase out of sight, I dashed towards the nearest bottle of milk. I was just about to bend down and take the bottle when the door to the house opened and a middle-aged woman appeared, collecting her pint of milk. My heart hammered in my chest. Worried that she had clocked what I had been about to do, I forced myself to continue walking, keeping the same pace. Luckily, she must have been too sleepy and distracted to notice me. When the door closed behind her once more, I breathed a sigh of relief. Grabbing the nearest bottle of milk, I raced back to my suitcase.

At once, I realised what a terrible thing I had done. I had stolen something from another person – I was a thief! Riddled with guilt, I began to feel hunted. Someone must have seen me committing my small, desperate crime. I would be pursued like the criminal I was. The police would be out looking for me – and it wouldn't take them long to track me down. After all, I stood out like a sore thumb: a vagrant wandering the streets with a suitcase.

I became convinced that I would end up in prison – and all because I had missed a coach. I had to conceal the evidence. Finding a discarded newspaper on the ground, I wrapped the bottle of milk in it, taking care not to leave so much as a sliver of glass showing. Only then did I dare to sample my ill-gotten gains.

All thought of guilt went straight out of my head. Every mouthful of that gold-topped full-cream milk tasted like the nectar of the gods, and I felt stronger and more confident, refreshed and ready to face the long day ahead.

When I had finished every last drop of that precious liquid, I looked around for a way to dispose of the bottle. Using the sleeve of my shirt, I carefully wiped the fingerprints off the glass before throwing it away – I had been reduced to thinking like a hardened criminal. Ashamed, I thought about my parents and my grandmother – what would they think about my behaviour? They would be horrified. I had been brought up properly and taught never to steal, no matter the circumstances; I had brought shame on my whole family.

Then, my thoughts turned to the occupants of the house I had stolen my pint of milk from. Who were they? Did they have work? Was it a big family? A houseful of hungry mouths? Were they poor? Could they afford to lose a pint of milk? These questions rattled around my head all day, and I resolved to remember the address and send the cost of the pint of milk to the occupants as soon as I got home.

My head held low, I looked for a place away from the town and the scene of my crime. I found a quiet, secluded park and retreated into it, staying put for most of the morning.

As soon as I had built up enough courage, I headed for the coach station, which I had already passed several times as I navigated the city. My first idea was to try to transfer my return ticket home. Unfortunately, the ticket I had booked ahead of time was valid for the Saturday only, and the coach company refused to help at all. Things were looking worse and worse. What was I to do?

Remembering what my grandmother had said about looking on the bright side of things, I felt in my pocket for the two shillings and sixpence I had found the day before in the bushes. At least I could purchase some food – something I badly needed by that point. I went to the cheapest shop I could find, but I was still only able to afford a loaf of bread, some margarine and three tomatoes. It was better than nothing – another observation my gran would undoubtedly have made – and I relished every bite.

Now that I was a wanted felon, I felt safer in the park, away from the patrolling police, so I returned to it for my third cold, uncomfortable night. By then, I felt like I could have slept anywhere. I sat on my suitcase, away from the damp grass, sheltered by the branches of a tree. Scant shelter it provided from the freezing cold, though. It was unusually bad weather for June, but perhaps I am remembering it unfavourably since it was such a low point in my life.

Eventually, I must have dropped off, for during the night I awoke to discover that it was raining heavily. The wind had blown up and I was in the middle of a storm – a real midsummer howler. Soaked to the skin, I had no choice but to emerge from the park and try my luck in the shop doorway again. My shoes were full of water and making terrible squelching noises. Drenched from head to toe, I felt like I might freeze to death.

I ducked into the lee of the window display, where there was some relief from the elements. After towelling myself down as best I could and trying to find something dry to wear in my suitcase, I began to feel quite depressed about the situation. I thought about admitting myself to hospital – I certainly felt ill enough. I imagined that I had pneumonia and it would be the end of me. The cold and wet had climbed right inside my bones.

In the midst of this, a policeman appeared – the same one as the night before, as it happened. My initial reaction was fear. I thought this was it – my crime had been discovered and now this upholder of the law had come to arrest me. I was fully prepared to hand myself over – particularly as it would be warmer in the cells than it was in the shop doorway. Perhaps the police would give me a cup of tea while they were filling out the paperwork at the station.

To my surprise, instead of clapping me in irons, the policeman peered at me through the rain and said, "Are you still here? I told you to move on."

On my own in the park, I had been allowing my imagination to get the better of my common sense. No one had seen me take that bottle of milk. This constable simply wanted to keep his patch clear of trouble.

With some relief, I explained my situation (leaving out the part about the milk bottle) and the policeman's demeanour immediately changed.

"Come on," he said, helping me to my feet. "You can't sleep here, mate. Head down to the police station when it opens first thing tomorrow morning. Tell them what you just told me and they'll get in touch with the police in Slough, who can contact your parents. They'll send you some money for your return ticket home. You'll be alright."

I was flooded with relief. My knees felt weak from sheer gratitude.

My parents transferred the money I needed to a bank in Liverpool. There were still several hours to wait before my coach was due to leave (and there was no way on Earth I was going to miss this one), so I found a church with an open door. Slipping inside, I prayed to God for forgiveness for my actions. Try as I might, I could not find a collection box, so I left the money for the milk I'd stolen on the altar. I could not bring myself to go back to the house I had taken it from.

As the coach from Liverpool sped homewards, I looked out of the back window, watching the city of my nightmare disappearing in the distance. I have never been so relieved to leave a place in my entire life.

A famous saying goes, "Give a man a fish, and you will feed him for a day. Teach a man to fish, and you will feed him for life."

My episode in Liverpool left me with a burning desire to start a charity for the homeless. Most homeless charities feed a person a fish for a day, as it were, rather than looking at the bigger picture and trying to set them up for their future. The charity I wish to champion will focus on teaching skills to the homeless so they can regain their independence and learn to fend for themselves.

It seems the Universe had a purpose for making me suffer on the streets of an unfamiliar city after all.

My first girlfriend

I had heard a great deal about the London ballrooms, like the *Hammersmith Palladium* and the *Locarno* in Streatham, but my favourite was the *Lyceum* just off the Strand, where Oscar Rabin and his band played every Saturday night. It was all very exciting and new – it seemed to me that there was a much more sophisticated kind of girl in the London clubs than there had been in Slough.

One young lady in particular captured my attention. She was stunning, bearing a striking resemblance to the film star Kim Novak, but one look at her told me I was out of my depth. I was afraid to approach her for fear of being rejected, so I decided I needed some Dutch courage in order to ask her to dance.

I headed to the bar and had a quick whisky to steel my nerves before returning to my previous post, from where I could observe her without attracting too much attention. During my brief time at the bar, she had been approached by another man, whom she had rejected. I hesitated, trying to decide whether I should or shouldn't ask her to dance. Although dancing with her was an attractive prospect, being turned down and rejected was not.

Despite the risk of humiliation and embarrassment, I made up my mind to do it anyway. It felt as though the eyes of every person in the ballroom were on me as I walked across the dance floor, though this was probably my imagination. This young woman was the centre of attention and astronomically out of my league, but to my complete astonishment, she agreed to dance with me. I could not believe my luck.

It struck me at that moment that my gran was right. I *could* do anything I put my mind to, including dancing with the most beautiful girl in the *Lyceum*.

Her name was Margaret, and she was very chatty and pleasant company, putting me immediately at my ease. We spent the rest of the evening together, much to my delight, and I walked her to Charing Cross Tube station where she would get the last train home to Eltham. We talked as we walked, and I found that we shared a keen interest in modern jazz.

Margaret worked at the University College Hospital in Gower Street as a secretary to one of the professors there. She was intelligent, beautiful, funny and kind – never in my wildest dreams had I thought I would one day be walking out with such a lovely person. She agreed to meet me for a date the following Tuesday, and I could hardly wait to spend more time with her. Three days to go, and I was counting them down. I was both excited and nervous at the same time.

Our first date consisted of a walk in St James's Park, where we talked for about three hours without stopping. We had so much to say to one another. It turned out that we had more in common than I had initially guessed as Margaret was also keen on motor racing, and she made me feel happy and relaxed. At the same time, I couldn't help but notice other men admiring her beauty and staring at the two of us. It certainly made me feel like I was the lucky one.

Whatever does she see in me? I wondered as I headed home that night.

The relationship quickly blossomed. Because of the distance between Margaret's home in Eltham and where I lived in Slough, it was not possible to meet up as often as we would have liked, so we kept in touch via letters and telephone. I always got excited when the postman arrived with her next letter. It was an innocent and pure relationship; she and I were brought up to save sex until after marriage, but we both knew it was true love.

Jazz at the Philharmonic

At the time, *Jazz at the Philharmonic*, an exciting performance produced by Norman Granz, was a major event in the modern jazz calendar, which attracted a varied line-up of artists and sold out weeks ahead of time. I was extremely lucky to obtain two tickets – one for me and one for Margaret – for one particular event at the famous *Gaumont State* in Kilburn, London – one of the larger venues *Jazz at the Philharmonic* played.

When the big day came, the *Gaumont State*, which had a capacity of four thousand, was full to bursting. Celebrities and modern jazz musicians who weren't working or on tour rubbed shoulders with excited music fans like Margaret and me. Everyone wanted to be at the heart of the action. It was a magical experience.

In the foyer after the show, among the famous faces milling around, I saw Ted Heath and Johnny Dankworth. Margaret, an excited flush on her face, told me giddily she had just spotted Hardy Krüger, the German film star. Her transformation into a love-struck schoolgirl rather took me by surprise and I wondered whether she was playing games with me, trying to make me jealous.

When she pointed her crush out to me, I realised that she had made an innocent mistake – it wasn't Hardy Krüger at all, but a friend of mine, Tony. It was easy to see how she had got them confused, particularly as he did bear a passing resemblance to the heartthrob and there were so many famous faces in the foyer that night. Since I was convinced she was toying with me, I decided to play a little game with her and wind her up.

"Oh yes, I see who you mean," I said. "Actually, I know him rather well. He's an old friend of mine."

Of course, Margaret didn't believe me. She told me that if we were friends, I could introduce them. I wound her up even more, pretending to hesitate, pleading social decorum and claiming it would be rude to intrude on him during his leisure time. It was obvious that she fancied Hardy Krüger, and that she still believed Tony was the real deal.

Annoyed, she accused me of lying to her about the man she had seen – the man she believed was Hardy Krüger – being my friend. Nobody calls me a liar! Margaret kept on and on about this bloody German film star for the rest of the evening and I was quite relieved when we lost sight of Tony in the crowd. By this point, I wanted to own up and admit that the person we had seen *was* my friend, but was definitely not a film star. However, before I had a chance to get a word in edgeways, she challenged me to arrange a double-date with 'Hardy Krüger' and her friend Barbara. Trying not to laugh as I still held the ace card – my very real friendship with Krüger lookalike Tony – I kept up the bluff, saying that I couldn't guarantee that he would be free since he was such a busy man.

"Why can't you just be honest with me, instead of making up these silly stories?" Margaret snapped. "I don't find it at all amusing."

I did, and her accusation that I was lying to her still rankled. Later that night, when I got home from the concert, I phoned Tony and asked him if he fancied a blind date with Margaret's friend, Barbara. At first he was reluctant, so I told him that if Barbara was anything like Margaret, he would be in for a pleasant surprise. When I had finally convinced Tony to agree, feeling pleased with myself, I telephoned Margaret to tell her the good news: the double-date was arranged for the following Sunday.

On the drive up to London to pick up the girls, I let Tony in on the scheme and we laughed at his attempts to impersonate Hardy Krüger. His German accent was atrocious, and we were hampered by the fact that neither of us had heard of Hardy Krüger before Margaret had mentioned him. I began to feel that perhaps this set-up hadn't been such a good idea after all. The whole thing had the potential to backfire on me in the worst way – I was already in Margaret's bad books, and I had no intention of humiliating her. I was in love with her and didn't want to lose her.

I told Tony to wait five minutes before coming to join us, giving me time to go on ahead to prepare the ground. Tony was to use the additional time to get into his role before speaking, and I wanted to see Margaret's reaction when he slowly appeared in the distance.

It worked like a charm. The look on her face was a picture of disbelief, shock, and then embarrassment as she realised the man she had seen at the *Gaumont State* – the man I had truthfully said was a friend of mine – may look like the famous German film star, but he obviously wasn't Hardy Krüger. Stunned, she made a valiant attempt to recover quickly so as not to look like a fool in front of her friend.

For her part, Barbara was still fooled as Tony came into sight. I could see it on her face and in her body language – she was fairly wetting herself with excitement. The nearer he got, the more I wondered what was going to happen – would the ladies laugh it off, or would this turn out to be a full-scale disaster? Surely Margaret would see the funny side of things? After all, I had never actually said that Hardy Krüger was my friend in so many words.

Fortunately, the ladies took the joke with good grace and the double-date turned out to be a resounding success. Tony and Barbara got on like a house on fire and we had a great time together. Later, Margaret even apologised for the mistake she had made and accusing me of telling fibs.

As my gran would have said, "Never jump to conclusions."

Changes

Margaret and I continued to see each other on a regular basis and were blissfully happy together. After about two years, our relationship was going from strength to strength, and she told me she would like to get engaged.

The thought of such a huge commitment terrified me. It was as if we had suddenly gone far too far down a path I hadn't intended to take. I thought we were too young to be settling down – we were only just in our twenties and had our whole lives ahead of us. Time and time again, I had seen school chums getting their girlfriends pregnant and having to tie the knot in a shotgun wedding, and it never ended well. For a time they would struggle on together, desperately trying to make ends meet, only for the whole thing to fall apart in a lengthy and unpleasant divorce. I didn't want that for Margaret and me – and I told her as much.

Margaret used to confide in an older work colleague who was always ready to listen – and to dispense advice. This interfering woman put it into Margaret's head that if I wasn't prepared to commit at that moment, then perhaps I wasn't as invested in the relationship as Margaret was. She suggested that we ought to separate for three months and have no contact with one another. Neither of us wanted to put this silly plan into action as we were both very much in love, but it seemed like the work colleague had some kind of hold over Margaret. Eventually she gave in and set a date for our separation.

After we separated, my first thought was how to pass the time for three months. Bored and missing Margaret, I slipped back into the familiar Slough dance club scene, and before long, I almost inevitably slipped into another relationship, too.

Sandy (not her real name) was nothing like Margaret. She had long brown hair, usually done up in a beehive, and tended to wear short skirts and tight sweaters. She oozed sex appeal. I had been a virgin when I'd met Sandy, but I had no intention of declining her sexual advances. She was no match for Margaret as far as I was concerned, but she helped me pass the long three months we spent apart.

I missed Margaret terribly during that time and was tempted to phone her on several occasions, but I never did. If I had given in, that would have been a sign of weakness, breaking our agreed rules.

Oh, how I longed for the time to pass.

As my wise old gran would remind me, "You never know what you've got until you lose it." She would also, no doubt, have advised me to save myself for Margaret rather than taking the easy option of spending my time with Sandy, just as she had advised me to save my money for the important things that I really wanted. However, sex was one aspect of my life I wasn't about to share with the redoubtable Granny Fraser!

Meanwhile, Sandy was becoming a habit. One particular so-called 'friend' – let's call him Steve – was constantly trying to encourage me to get engaged to her, saying, "You must get a ring on her finger before you lose her."

It wasn't long before I discovered Steve's true colours – he wanted to keep Sandy and me together while he turned on the charm and wormed himself into Margaret's affections. As soon as I found out, I knew I could no longer trust him as a friend, but by then the damage had been done. Not only had he been encouraging me to make things more permanent with Sandy, he had also been going behind my back and telling Margaret that I was seeing another woman.

Three months passed and I was relieved to be able to see my darling Margaret again. We met at the time we had agreed before the separation, but because of Steve's foul play, she was terribly upset with me. She said she could never trust me again, that I had betrayed her. I was devastated.

As I tried to pick up my life and move on, Steve, I'm happy to report, got nowhere with Margaret. Serves him right! However, I still look back from time to time and wonder how different my life might have been if I had married Margaret when I had the chance. It just goes to show that although I could get whatever I wanted if I put my mind to it, I could just as easily lose it if I allowed my resolve to waver.

Growing Up and Moving On

The Yellow Door

In 1957, I was out with three friends. Chris was driving a pink Vauxhall Cresta with Tony next to him on the bench seat in the front of the car, and I was in the back with Dicky. As we drove past our local coffee bar, *The Yellow Door* – a regular meeting place for all our friends, I decided to get out of the car. I asked Chris to stop and arranged to meet up with him and the others later. When I got out, Dicky hopped in the front with Tony – there were no seatbelts in those days, so the passengers could squeeze in together on the bench seat.

I had been in the coffee bar for about twenty minutes when word came through that there had been a terrible accident involving a pink Vauxhall Cresta. I just knew this was Chris's car – who else would have a pink Cresta? The accident must have happened minutes after I'd got out of the car.

I rushed to the scene. By the time I got there, the police had closed the road and the ambulance had already gone. I did not know if my friends were alive or dead.

The crash scene made me feel physically sick – my friends' shoes were scattered all over the road. But when I saw the wreck of the car, I was in for an even worse shock. The back of it was practically flat. If Dicky and I had been in the back seat when the car had crashed, we would have been crushed.

My immediate emotions upon seeing the devastation were shock and horror. I was convinced that no one could possibly have survived such an awful crash – my three friends had to be dead. Luckily, though, I was wrong.

Because they had all been sitting so close together and not wearing seatbelts, Chris, Dicky and Tony had been thrown clear of the car. Though they still suffered life-threatening injuries, this had saved their lives. I shook my head as I walked away, knowing that it could have been me being taken to the hospital in an ambulance along with my friends, but in actual fact, things could have been so much worse. The crash investigators said later that had I stayed in the car, Tony and Chris probably wouldn't have been thrown clear, and Dicky and I would have been squashed flat.

Looking back, I can see that my decision to get out at *The Yellow Door* probably saved all our lives. Shortly before the accident, I had been riding in that car with no intention of getting out. It was entirely beyond my control, of course, so I shouldn't take all the credit. My guardian angel was certainly looking over me that day.

This was a true miracle that I am thankful for to this day.

Taking the plunge

Towards the end of my time with the company which believed it had Sir Hugh Fraser's son managing its biggest shop in the country, I had a call from a friend of mine. My old boss, Monty, was very ill with heart problems, and his doctor had advised him to sell his shop and take it easy. I went to visit him, and he suggested that I should buy the shop along with the large house next door.

At that time, a friend of mine worked for his father's firm of solicitors. We would meet most lunchtimes for a quick half and talk about everything from girls to golf. After having visited Monty and heard his proposal, I mentioned it to my friend over lunch the next time we met, saying it was out of the question. Since Monty knew me so well, it made sense for him to offer me first refusal when the time came to sell his business, but I simply didn't have the kind of money that he was asking for. However, I had to admit that the thought of working for myself held a certain glamour.

My friend quite by chance was going to be passing the property that afternoon, and he offered to take a look. Later that same day, he came into my shop and told me there was no reason not to buy it – it was a good business and the buildings were sound. When I reminded him about my lack of funds, he said that wouldn't be a problem. He could deal with the mortgage – it was the field he specialised in, after all.

I was elated to know that I would soon be the owner of a successful business and valuable real estate, and I felt a great deal of pride when I was able to break the news to my parents. I had achieved something they had only dreamed of. Having worked so many hours for Monty, I knew his shop and house well, so I knew exactly what needed to be done in order to bring them up to scratch, and I was well-qualified to run the business.

I soon settled into my new self-employed lifestyle, working in my very own shop. My days were spent serving, stacking shelves, cleaning, making up orders, accepting deliveries, and carrying out general maintenance to keep things ticking along satisfactorily. It was a world apart from what I had become used to – working for a chain of businesses as part of a team who all pulled together. Right at the sharp end of running a small business, I now had the responsibility of making all the decisions, paying wages, ordering stock, paying the bills, balancing the books, and trying to make a profit. In the fruit and vegetable trade, much of the stock has a very short shelf life, which was a bit of a shock for someone who was used to working with cars. If I wasn't careful, I could find myself throwing away my entire profit margin in the form of spoiled food.

I was on my own, with no one to fall back on, worrying about whether or not I could make sufficient profits each month to pay the large mortgage I had taken out in order to purchase the two properties. Although I soon grew tired of seeing the same customers' faces every day, I was glad when they came through the door as they meant I could pay the bills.

Mrs O's big idea

After the novelty of being my own boss had worn off, which didn't take nearly as long as I'd thought it would, I realised that I had rather rashly given up the security of a good, well-paid job to work in a corner shop. Listening to the locals gossip all day is a decent enough way to make a living, and I've no doubt another person would have thoroughly enjoyed it, but it did nothing for me. I had to make small-talk and be pleasant to people I barely knew, some of whom I didn't like at all, which felt false. It didn't sit well with me.

I owned a convenience store, and that was all it was. Most of my customers would do their regular shopping at the supermarkets, and only popped into my store to pick up anything they may have forgotten. The only way I could compete was to keep long, tiring hours. In those days, most shops closed at six o'clock, with half-day closing in mid-week and no trading on a Sunday. I had to keep my shop open when the others were shut – there was no way I could ever have competed on price.

I was living in the six-bedroomed house next door to the shop, which was far too big for one person and could be lonely and stressful at times. Making myself as comfortable as I could, I had one bedroom, a kitchen and a bathroom to myself, but it was like living in a warehouse, with boxes everywhere. I couldn't move for clutter, and there were bits and pieces of furniture all over the building. However, I didn't have time to sort it all out; I was too busy working in the shop. I employed two part-timers for the busy periods, but most of the time I worked alone.

One of my regulars, Mrs O, was always coming up with ideas for the big house. She thought it was a beautiful house, and complained that it was such a waste for so many of its rooms to be empty. When she suggested that I let the rooms to students, I did a few calculations and realised that she was on to something. Using the surplus food from the shop to feed my guests, I could make more profit from letting rooms than I could from retail. With the short shelf life of the food I was selling, it made a lot of sense to combine the shop with a cooked food-led business (bed, breakfast and evening meal).

Mrs O transformed one of the rooms into a twin room to use as a pilot scheme, and it worked well. Within two months, I had converted all six bedrooms into letting rooms. After a lot of hard work getting each room shipshape and Bristol fashion for letting, I then learned how to cook. My breakfasts became renowned for being the best in the area, and I would prepare the food for the evening meal in my lunch hour. Mrs O was always there to lend a hand.

Due to the huge demand for student accommodation, I decided to extend the property. I had plans drawn up for a five-bedroom extension, which were passed by the Council Planning Department. Now all I had to do was find a decent builder.

In the property business, there is always some maintenance to be done, whether it be a small repair or a large extension. People use buildings and cause wear and tear, even when they are careful. In my case, it felt like a natural progression to expand my skills into the building trade. I had had plenty of practice in my teenage years, helping Monty with his DIY projects – I was good at painting and decorating, and I had even managed to pick up a little carpentry along the way.

Soon, I was turning my hand to every trade I could imagine. I even rewired a room to increase the number of available plug sockets, which, looking back, was pushing it for an amateur. Although nobody was ever electrocuted by my wiring, I probably should have left it to the professionals and called a qualified electrician in.

Silver linings

In life, great things often come about as the result of chance encounters. I would never have met my good friend Colin if it hadn't been for a piece of misfortune.

Around the time I was planning my extension, I had a break-in at the shop. The thieves took my entire cigarette stock and left considerable damage, and the break-in made the search for a builder all the more urgent. There were so many to choose from in the *Yellow Pages*, so eventually I took a pin and chose one at random.

Colin turned up promptly and did the necessary work to secure the shop. I was impressed at the quality and speed of his work, so over a coffee, we discussed my plans for the extension. He agreed to do the work for a reasonable price, providing I supplied the materials and worked as his labourer. This worked well as I managed to get a lot of the material from local demolition sites, which helped me keep to my tight budget.

Colin was a godsend. What he didn't know about the building trade wasn't worth knowing, and after ten months of working as his labourer, I had picked up a lot of his knowledge. He knew my financial position and helped all he could, never harassing me for money. Conscientious about getting building materials for the right price, he had contacts with good tradesmen, plumbers and electricians.

Colin and I would socialise on a regular basis and soon became good friends. He had a great sense of humour and was always a pleasure to be around. There was never a problem with maintenance, either, as Colin was always on hand – even in the middle of the night for emergencies.

I recall an occasion during a torrential downpour when water was pouring through the roof and into one of the guest bedrooms, the result of a broken roof tile that had been overlooked. That was the kind of issue that couldn't wait until the morning, so as soon as I spotted it, I called Colin immediately, even though it was something like three in the morning.

By the time he arrived, I had managed to move the bed out of the way and get buckets under the leak before it could cause any further damage. Colin turned the water off and took an initial look at what he needed to do to fix the problem, then he was back first thing in the morning, spending most of the day sorting out the roof. He never complained about the late (or early) hour of an emergency call; he simply turned up and got on with the job, never letting me down. He would turn his hand to anything, even helping in the guesthouse on occasions.

Colin was what I call a real friend.

Six loaves of bread

By the time the extension was complete and ready for business, the demand for student accommodation had dried up. I was struggling to let the rooms and found myself in a lot of debt.

Another of my regulars in the corner shop, Mr P, had a standing order for six sliced loaves of white bread every day. Sometimes, he would collect them from the house after I had closed the shop. He rarely bought anything else, and I often wondered what they were for. I imagined he must have a very large family.

After about two years, Mr P told me he was emigrating to Australia and had to cancel his order. At the same time, he asked me if I wanted to buy any furniture. I arranged to meet him that evening at his house, and when I got there, I couldn't believe my eyes. He lived in a very large house, and every dormitory-style room, each sleeping six people, was fully let.

Intrigued to know the secret of his success, I asked how he managed to keep his rooms full. It turned out that he had a contract to take in workers from the local Ford commercial factory. As the student market had completely dried up, it did not take me long to see the value in the lucrative market of letting rooms to contract workers.

I contacted the Personnel Officer at the Ford factory and he agreed to transfer Mr P's contract to me, so I used the furniture from Mr P's house to furnish the rooms ready for my new guests. The Personnel Officer would phone me every Monday morning to ask how many vacancies I had, as that was when he had to find accommodation for the new recruits, and as a result, my rooms were always full.

Who would have thought that my curiosity over a daily order for six loaves of bread would lead me to a solution to my lack of lettings? Once again, although I still had no idea of the concept at the time, the Law of Attraction had worked in my favour.

What a Carry On

In 1969, I was having a drink with Colin at one of our local haunts in Windsor. Spotting a 'For Sale' sign as we passed a derelict house on our way home, I asked Colin whether he would like to work on it. He said he would love to, so we stopped to take a closer look. However, we couldn't see further than the front door – the building was boarded up and a large notice read, "Do not enter, dangerous property".

I had noticed this property in the past, but I'd never seen a 'For Sale' sign before. I contacted the estate agent the following day to get the details of the property and make further enquiries. The house had been empty for years, and thanks to a damaged and leaking roof, it was now in a sorry state. It was riddled with dry rot, wet rot and woodworm. Colin reckoned that the best thing to do would be to demolish it and start again.

It couldn't be mortgaged, so I put in a silly offer of £950. To my amazement, it was accepted. The condition of the property had put most buyers off, and as it was an executor's sale, the vendors wanted a quick sale to avoid it becoming a liability.

The house was a Victorian mansion with eight bedrooms, a lot of original features, and high ceilings. Sadly, the ceilings would have to be replaced because of the water damage, but I saw it as an opportunity.

Work on the house started in the winter of 1969, which was a particularly lean time – especially in the building trade. As a result of this, Colin didn't have a great deal of work on, and he had to allocate his jobs carefully in order to be able to support himself and his family. They were his source of income, after all; he was only getting mates' rates for the jobs he did for me.

Colin would arrive at my guesthouse to pick me up, mucking in in the kitchen until I had finished cooking and serving breakfast. We would then grab some breakfast for ourselves and drive over to the house. It was an astonishingly cold winter that year, so our first job of the day would be to build a small, manageable fire in the garden to burn all the rotten timber we were pulling out of the old house. The heat from the fire was warmer than the cold, crumbling shell of a house, so needless to say, we both looked forward to huddling round it for tea breaks and lunch.

One morning, when we arrived to work on the house, much to our surprise, we discovered the road leading up to it was closed. After some investigation, we found out that a film crew, complete with actors, cameramen, sound engineers – the works, was using the adjoining land to film *Carry On Up the Jungle*. The whole road had been turned into a working film set and it was a hive of activity, strewn with catering vehicles, mobile dressing rooms, prop cases, the props themselves – everything you may imagine a film crew would need to record a couple of scenes.

Of course, this was all very interesting, but we had a job to do. Finally, we managed to convince the film crew to let us through. It wasn't an unreasonable request, since they were obstructing the entire road.

The kind of renovation we were undertaking on the house generated a lot of noise – banging nails into the floorboards, sawing wood, and so on. As we threw ourselves into the work with renewed vigour, anxious to make up for the delay we'd encountered in persuading the film crew to let us pass, the noise levels increased until we could barely hear ourselves think.

Suddenly, we were interrupted by a bellow from the open front door. The film crew boss was calling up to us, explaining that his team couldn't get any work done with all the noise we were making. Taken by surprise, we stopped, and that put paid to that morning's work. We did try to do quiet jobs to fill the time, but after a while, we couldn't put laying more floorboards off any longer.

Attempting to judge when the film crew would be taking a break for lunch, we started with our banging and hammering again. This time, we were half prepared for a showdown, and sure enough, the boss appeared at the door again. After lots of angry shouting, we found ourselves at a bit of an impasse.

Luckily, the film crew boss was a reasonable man. After having a look around, he realised that he would be costing us money by preventing us from working, so he offered to pay us £100 to stop the job for one day. In 1969, £100 was a lot of money, so we could hardly refuse such a generous offer. And he wasn't to know that it was only the two of us on site. Happily splitting the money in two, we found a few more quiet things to do on the property then went home, both having made a profit for the day even though we'd hardly got any work done.

The hotel in Windsor

Our first job on the derelict house had been to fix the roof, replacing any rotten timbers and making it weatherproof. Most of the interior had to be gutted and we burned a lot of the timber in the garden. Once we had stripped and cleared the house, we were ready to start restoring it to its former glory.

As usual, we went to local demolition sites to find replacement timber. I had to get the sash windows made up especially, but once again, Colin had the right contact at the right price. Each joist was carefully examined, de-nailed, and treated with creosote at the ends which were to be inserted into the brickwork. We were determined to rebuild the house so well that it would last for many years to come, and the quality of the materials we were using was often better than the originals had been.

I learned about the hotel and catering industry by taking classes at night school, then working for two seasons in a hotel in Jersey. The opportunities and experience I gained during my time in Jersey were invaluable to me, even though the work was akin to slave labour. I would get up at 6.30am to scrub the marble steps leading up to the main entrance, water the plants, then tidy and clean the front of the hotel and the pavement adjoining it. I had to make the hotel entrance look spic and span, open and inviting to holidaymakers. In the hotel trade, appearances – and first impressions in particular – are very important.

After my cleaning duties, I would run up to my room and change into waiting clothes in order to fulfil my restaurant duties during the breakfast rush. When breakfast was finished, I would head into the kitchen to help the chef prepare the vegetables for lunch and dinner. My long morning shift would finish at 3pm, then I had a two-hour break. I was usually so exhausted, I would just go up to my room and collapse on my bed until I had to be back on duty to look after new arrivals and prepare for the dinner service.

Needless to say, working this hellish shift pattern seven days a week, I didn't get as much time to enjoy the beach as I had hoped. It was worth it in the end, though. I made a reasonable wage, and because I was either working or asleep, I had no opportunity to spend any of it. And as my gran would have said, "Hard work never killed anybody." I was also lucky enough to be entitled to free food and accommodation for the duration of my contract – one of the perks of working in the hotel and catering business.

Another bonus of working so many hours was that I was generally on hand to meet and greet the guests. They would notice that I was always ready to help them, and as they were on holiday, and therefore in a generous mood, they would make sure to tip me well at the end of their stay. These tips went a long way to boosting my savings account.

Most importantly, my qualifications and the experience I gained by working in Jersey meant that when the time came to open the hotel in Windsor, I could command a much higher tariff than I had been charging at my B&B in Slough. The hotel was an immediate success, attracting a lot of foreign visitors – mostly Americans. Windsor being a tourist town, with the castle as the main attraction, the property was ideally positioned for a hotel, and its original features gave it a historical character.

It was then that I decided to lease my shop so I could concentrate on the hotel business full-time.

The perfect hotel

When I had been running both my letting property and the hotel in Windsor for two years, I decided that I was ready to move on to bigger and better things. Most of the big commercial estate agents were in London, and I would receive the details of six properties a day on average from the different agents I was registered with. A lot of these properties were unsuitable for what I had in mind, so I binned the details. The few properties that had potential I kept on my shortlist to view at a later date, sorting the list into regions covering the entire country. I knew exactly what I was looking for, but I couldn't seem to find it.

After months of disappointing viewings, I took to visiting the agents in person on a regular basis. One Friday, I was in the offices of one particular commercial estate agent in Hanover Square, Central London, having some trouble with the manager. Abrupt and unhelpful, he was telling me that I had seen everything on his books, and if I didn't believe him, I could look for myself.

I didn't believe him, so I took him up on his offer and went through the filing cabinet he had indicated. Right at the back was a file with the details of a hotel I had not seen before – he had never sent this file to me. What's more, it met all of my requirements. Unimpressed by his attitude, I got the manager to call the hotel to arrange for me to have a viewing the following Sunday.

The property was called Ragdale Hall and was situated near Melton Mowbray. I have always had a passion for old houses, but Ragdale Hall was different. I knew as soon as I looked at the sale details that it was the place I had been looking for all my life, without even knowing it. It was as though it was meant to be – and knowing what I know now about the Law of Attraction, I realise that it was indeed meant to be.

Ragdale Hall was set in nine glorious acres of land, proudly overlooking the surrounding farmland. It was an attractive property, even without the many unique and wonderful details like the clock tower with six chiming bells, or the period features – some dating back to when it was built by Robert Shirley, the Sixth Earl

Ferrers, in 1785. I knew if the walls could have talked, they would have had many an interesting tale to tell.

After the viewing, I could recall every detail of the property. I could not get it out of my head. The excitement I felt was almost overwhelming – I was finally putting the wheels of my latest plans in motion. I put my letting property, the hotel in Windsor, and the freehold for the shop up for sale, fearing all the time that somebody else would pip me to the post and snap Ragdale Hall up from under my nose.

Whatever the cost, I had to find a way for Ragdale Hall to be mine.

Ragdale Hall

The history of Ragdale Hall

The first large hall to be built on the site was known as Rakedale Old Hall, which burned to the ground in the mid-eighteenth century. The building that followed, commissioned by the Sixth Earl Ferrers, Robert Shirley, was constructed in stone and completed in 1785.

The Shirley family at that time was a little chaotic. The Earl's father had brought disgrace on the family by murdering his faithful servant, Johnson, at the family seat, Stanton Harrold, Leicestershire, in 1760. On 5 May 1760, he was executed for his crime – coincidentally, the last peer of the realm to be executed by hanging. Perhaps the Sixth Earl Ferrers wanted to distance himself from this scandal and its repercussions, as he subsequently moved his attention to what was to become Ragdale Hall.

In more modern times, Ragdale Hall became the home of

the Quorn Hunt, a particularly famous local hunt, in the 1930s. The pack is still maintained, though the dogs no longer actively hunt, and is rumoured to be one of the United Kingdom's oldest fox hunting packs – if not the world's oldest. All the bedrooms at Ragdale, instead of being numbered, have the names of local hunts: the Atherstone, the Blankley, the Cotterstone and the Quorn, to name but a few.

At the time that I was looking to purchase Ragdale Hall, the locals were eager to inform me of several scandals concerning Edward, the Eight Duke of Windsor, who had previously owned the property. Apparently, he had thought he had a way with the ladies – though possibly his position was more effective than his charms – and was rumoured to have fathered several illegitimate children in the local area before passing away on 28 May, 1972.

Out of nowhere

As enthused as I was about Ragdale Hall's past, I had to find a way to become a part of its future. I refused to give up, even when it seemed unlikely I would succeed. Every waking moment I spent thinking about the Hall; I poured all my energy into it. Memories of the viewing kept flooding back into my mind in colourful, vibrant detail. I lived and breathed that place – nothing else mattered to me.

I went to my bank to get a loan, but my bank manager turned me down. I tried several other potential moneylenders, but the result was always the same. It was beginning to seem as though it would be impossible for me to raise the money I needed for Ragdale Hall when I bumped into an old friend, Jerry, and happened to mention the difficulty I was having with my new venture.

Jerry was the sort of guy who no one took seriously, so when he told me not to worry, his bank manager would help me, I didn't entirely believe him. At this point, though, I was getting pretty desperate – I could not afford to leave any stone unturned, so I went along with his suggestion. Jerry made a call and arranged a meeting with the bank manager, who as it turned out was a good friend of his.

I thought it was strange that he had arranged for us all to meet in a pub, but this was typical of Jerry. Once the introductions were complete, the bank manager bought me a drink and told me that he had heard about my financial problems. Asking me to bring my business plan and cash flow forecast with me, he said he would happily discuss the finances with me at the bank the following day.

At 10am the next morning, feeling a little nervous, I arrived at the bank and went through the details of my business plan with the manager. He agreed to the loan in principle, subject to the bank's valuation – I could not believe my luck! I opened an account with his bank there and then, and deposited all the money from the sales of my properties and businesses.

Over the next few months, I became good friends with Dennis, the bank manager. As we were nearing the exchange of contracts for Ragdale Hall, I realised there would be a shortfall in the deposit I required. I was out one evening with my new friend Dennis, drinking champagne at *Bill Bentley's Oyster Bar*, when one of his customers came over to our table to say hello. After introducing us, Dennis promptly asked his customer to help me out, that I needed £10,000 to complete on a property deal. I was embarrassed, as you may imagine, but to my astonishment, on Dennis's say so, this man got out his cheque book and wrote me a cheque for £10,000.

Yes, this really did happen to me – more proof of the Law of Attraction at work on my behalf.

A bit of a hitch

Following the exchange of contracts, I lived at Ragdale Hall as a paying guest leading up to the completion of the sale. When that momentous day finally arrived, I had everything ready. The removal lorry arrived on time, waiting for the go-ahead from the solicitors.

To my horror, a phone call came through from the bank. The clerk told me that they could not release the money for Ragdale Hall as they had just discovered a legal charge on the property. It must have been a simple solicitor's error that this charge had been overlooked, but at the time it felt like a disaster. I was shocked and devastated, and for the next three days, I was unable to come to terms with the situation.

At the time, right at the beginning of the boom in 1972, property prices were rising weekly. The current owner of Ragdale Hall was unhelpful, refusing to give me any information, as it would have been to his advantage for the sale to be cancelled. He would then have been able to command a higher price from a new buyer. To compound matters, he served me with a notice to complete the sale of the property within twenty-one days or the contract would be rescinded. This placed me in an impossible situation. I felt as though the world was crashing down around me – I would lose everything if I couldn't complete within the given period.

While I was trying to work out what to do, I spent the evenings in the bar of Ragdale Hall, listening to the off-duty staff gossiping. I picked up a snippet of information that the owner of the hotel had had an affair with one of the waitresses, and it could be she who had put the legal charge on the property.

I called my solicitor and this suspicion was confirmed.

Time was running out fast, but I was on a mission. The lady in question lived in Ireland, and her daughter lived in Hinckley, Leicestershire. I had to contact the daughter to get her mother's address in Ireland, and after a brief phone call, she agreed to meet with me.

When I met the daughter, I sided with her mother, explaining that it would be in her best interests to finalise the long-standing charge. At first, the daughter rather looked down her nose at me with a 'What's in it for me?' attitude. I had to win her over – her cooperation was vital to my plan. Finally, she realised that what I wanted would ultimately benefit her mother, too, and her manner towards me changed.

Although she remembered the fling her mother had had with the owner of Ragdale Hall, she couldn't add anything further. However, she called her mother in Ireland and we both spoke with her. After a long conversation, the mother agreed to come over to the

UK to meet me, providing I paid the airfare.

By the time we had the meeting at her solicitor's office in Prestwick, Scotland, it was the final day of the time period the owner of Ragdale Hall had given me to complete the deal. I had until noon, and we met at 10am.

I waited anxiously in the waiting room while she took legal advice in her solicitor's office, experiencing all kinds of emotions and jumping at every small noise. This was the biggest gamble of my life to date – it would make or break my future. If I failed to pull this one off, I would lose everything in one fell swoop. The consequences did not bear thinking about. It was torture knowing that the moment of reckoning was coming, but not what the outcome might be. The only solace I had was that I would soon be put out of my misery, one way or the other.

The door to the solicitor's office finally opened and I was summoned inside. I made it quite clear that I was proposing a one-time only offer of £500 for her to relinquish the legal charge on the property and it was non-negotiable. I offered to sign a contract to the effect that she would not relinquish any claim that she had over the current owner, only the property.

I was ushered back into the waiting room while she discussed the matter with her solicitor. My whole future rested on her decision; I had done all that I could.

After what seemed like an eternity, the door to the solicitor's office opened again and in I went to receive some of the best new I have ever had – she had agreed to lift the legal charge on Ragdale Hall. I now had twenty minutes to complete the deal before the time ran out. Sweating and frantic, I called my solicitor in London to tell him the good news.

Finally, I was the proud owner of Ragdale Hall. Now a renowned health spa, back then, it was a hotel and restaurant, a wedding venue and country club. My first task was to bring it up to date by closing the country club and replacing it with a disco and live bands. This increased the takings substantially, and impressed my bank manager and friend, Dennis. He and his wife would visit on a regular basis, particularly enjoying the peaceful countryside surrounding the Hall, which was a far cry from the busy city life they were used to in London. My mother and father were both proud of me, too, watching me achieve things that hadn't been possible in their time because of the privations and austerity of the Second World War.

A flamboyant extrovert

It broke the mould when Martin (not his real name) was born – what a character he was. A one off, that's for sure.

I first met Martin in 1955 when we were both working in the rag trade as junior salesmen for Montague Burton, the gents' tailors. Even then, he showed a keen interest in the fashion of the day and always made the most of his modest wage to keep up a smart image. He dressed immaculately, never a hair out of place, and exuded confidence. Soon developing a style of his own, Martin really stood out from the crowd.

Martin never kept a job for long; he was restless, always on the lookout for the next challenge, the next adventure. He enjoyed living life to the full and needed stimulation, working as a manager at the local cinema, a butler, a chauffeur, and a house-sitter, among many other things. Often, he took domestic positions in large country houses and found himself with access to all the luxuries and amenities these places had to offer.

Martin also spent time in the Merchant Navy and travelled the globe, which suited his wanderlust perfectly. He and I kept in touch over the years, and we would often meet up for drinks and a catch up when he was in the UK. I loved listening to his stories of adventures on and off the high seas, and I think he enjoyed telling his tales as much as I enjoyed hearing them.

When I was nearing the completion of the purchase of Ragdale Hall, I met up with Martin for one of our usual get-togethers: a drink and a chat in a friendly pub. When I told him what I was up to, he offered his services as manager of Ragdale Hall. He had accumulated quite a bit of experience in the hospitality industry by then, and as I knew he was a person I could trust, I thought this was a great idea. Martin as manager would be a real asset while I was getting the business off the ground, enabling me to focus on the major decisions while he attended to the day-to-day running of the hotel.

It would turn out to be a steep learning curve for the both of us.

Panic!

I had to wait for the previous owner of Ragdale Hall to move out before I could move in, and this is when I saw his dark side. Believe me when I tell you I kept a watchful eye on him to make sure he only took his personal possessions with him. He had turned nasty by this point, angered by losing out on a higher price in a booming market, so I didn't want him touching any of the items listed on the sale inventory.

As I finally escorted him off the premises, he took the opportunity to steal the function book from the front desk. This held the dates, contact details and arrangements for all the upcoming events at Ragdale Hall, including business meetings, parties and weddings, and he knew that I could not run the business without it. There was a scuffle as I tried to prevent him from ruining my livelihood – and the livelihoods of the staff working at the Hall – but he knocked me to the ground and scarpered with the all-important function book.

I was livid. I went back inside, only to discover that the large stuffed black bear – a trophy from a hunt in days gone by – that had taken pride of place in the reception had also disappeared. I'll never know how he managed to sneak that one past me. Of course, I had no choice but to sue him. I won the case, but never recovered the function book. He had destroyed it out of pure spite.

Well, now I had a problem: six months' worth of bookings and no way to contact anybody to replace their lost details. I placed announcements in the *Leicester Mercury* and *Nottingham Post* explaining the situation and asking anybody with bookings to get in touch with us. There was nothing more I could do – I could only sit back and hope for the best to salvage what trade I could.

Fortunately, the adverts I placed in the local newspapers did their job. Over the coming weeks, the missing functions began to reappear, and the new function book was looking quite healthy. Relaxing a little, I allowed the reception desk staff to start taking new bookings again.

To my dismay, though, it wasn't all to be plain sailing from there. One Friday afternoon, a van drew up outside the hotel and a woman appeared from within it with a large number of boxes containing an enormous multi-tiered wedding cake. My heart sank – there was a wedding booked in for the next day, and we had no idea about it whatsoever. This was one booking that had slipped through the net – the organisers must have missed my advertisements.

I took the cake lady through to the reception lounge and explained the situation to her, and she filled me in on the details of the wedding we were supposed to be holding. It was a big affair, with 200 guests expecting a sit-down meal, not to mention the overnight accommodation for the bride and groom and their families. My face probably turned as white as a sheet as she was speaking – it was a terrifying prospect, putting together a lavish wedding in so short a time. It would be an unqualified disaster and Ragdale Hall's reputation for high standards would be at stake.

I called the mother of the bride from the details the cake lady had given me, and she came out to meet me. I had to tell her that it was impossible for Ragdale Hall to host the wedding – there was simply no way we could pull things together in such a short amount of time. For a start, we would be woefully short-staffed; the temporary function waitresses had to be booked months in advance, and they would all have been hired for other functions by now. The agency I used in Leicester was brilliant, and the Spanish lady who ran it had a bit of a soft spot for me – after all, it was a privilege to have Ragdale Hall as one of her contracts, but even that wouldn't be enough to conjure waitresses out of thin air.

The mother of bride broke down in tears. Family and friends were travelling to Ragdale Hall from all over the world; the following day was supposed to be the happiest day of her daughter's life. Even though she was distressed, she was a reasonable woman and understood that we were not to blame.

I felt terribly sorry for her and wanted to help her as much as I could. In the end, I agreed to try my best to put the wedding plans together for the happy couple, but I warned her that I could not guarantee Ragdale Hall's usual high standards, given the short notice. She thanked me profusely as I assured her that we would do our best, then I sprinted back inside as soon as she was out of sight. We were really up against it on this one.

There was a Friday night disco that evening so we wouldn't be able to begin preparing the room for the wedding until after it had finished – and that was at 1am. When I called an emergency staff meeting, I can't say that everyone was enthusiastic about the prospect of working through the night, but they didn't want to let the bride and groom and their families down, or the reputation of Ragdale Hall. The wedding was supposed to begin at 3pm the following day; we had fewer than twenty-four hours.

It was all systems go. I remember running around, along with the rest of my staff, in a state of barely controlled panic. Calling the mother of the bride, I agreed a new menu with her – I think she was so relieved that the wedding could go ahead that she would have agreed to almost anything. The head chef made a list of all the supplies he needed, and I then spent a good hour ringing around my suppliers – butchers, fishmongers, wine merchants and florists. They were all a bit stunned as they had never before experienced panic coming from Ragdale Hall, but they agreed to do what they could. However, there were still items missing from the chef's list. Somehow – and to this day, I'm not sure how – I managed to get to the cash and carry before it closed for the night.

Next was the issue of staff. As I had predicted, all our usual temporary function staff were already employed elsewhere that Saturday, so I ran round to our neighbouring pub and restaurant, The Durham Ox. The manager, John, and I were good friends – thank God. As soon as he heard my predicament, he lent me the extra staff I needed.

Of course, weddings aren't just about food and staff; there were 100 other loose ties to bring together. Try as I might, I couldn't find a photographer at such short notice. Thinking on my feet, I put out an emergency appeal on the local radio, and to my immense relief, someone got in touch. He must have been the only wedding photographer not already employed that weekend.

I checked in on the kitchen situation: it was a hive of slightly stressed activity, but it was running like a well-oiled machine. Next was the function room. It would have to be the largest function room in the hotel in order to cope with 200 wedding guests, but that meant we had to wait for the Friday night disco to finish and the last partygoers to leave. In the meantime, we prepared empty rooms for the guests the mother of the bride had told me would be staying over on Saturday night.

At last, the disco finished and the small army of staff I had managed to pull together swarmed into the ballroom. It was a big clean-up operation since it was such a large room, then we had to cover the dancefloor (it would be uncovered again after the wedding dinner for the guest to dance) and set out tables. The flowers arrived at dawn, when I was forced to send some of my exhausted and aching colleagues off to prepare breakfast and deal with the everyday running of the hotel.

I have no idea how we managed it, but by 2pm, when the wedding guests began to arrive and gather in the bar, we had transformed the ballroom into a beautiful, elegant wedding venue. It looked truly stunning. By then, all of us were on our knees with exhaustion. We had time to grab a bite to eat and a cup of tea before freshening up ready for the event itself.

With the exception of the mother of the bride (who assured me of her eternal gratitude), none of the guests had any idea of the panic that had gone on through the night. We had done the impossible – and we had pulled it off in a professional manner. I was extremely proud of my team that day.

The Aston Martin Owners' Club
The staff at Ragdale Hall really could work wonders, so if there wasn't a function to prepare for and we weren't busy in the hotel,

I would treat them to a few drinks in the bar with the customers. The only rule I had was that we all remained presentable and reasonably upright.

I recall partying with the customers and having too much to drink well into the early hours of one particular Sunday morning. Sundays ran later than other days, even when it came to the breakfast service, so the staff could afford to have a lie-in as long as the phone and reception were covered. Sometimes, we would draw lots for those particular honours, but usually one or two people wanted an earlier night than the rest of us, so they were happy to volunteer. This arrangement worked well for everyone.

That Sunday morning, however, the receptionist woke me from a dead sleep at half past nine. Although I was bleary-eyed and a little the worse for drink, it dawned on me that she was panicking – and this was a woman not normally given to panic. She explained that there were customers downstairs – and lots of them.

I dressed quickly before shaking Martin awake. Leaving him to rouse the rest of the staff and get them on duty before the people downstairs realised anything was wrong, I did my best to hide my dazed, half-awake expression from the customers and made some subtle investigations.

This was another booking that had fallen through the net. It was the Aston Martin Owners' Club annual meeting, and – to my mounting horror – it was to include breakfast. Luckily, it wasn't scheduled to begin until ten, so I had a few minutes to bluff my way through.

The restaurant dining room was already prepared for Sunday lunch, but luckily we only had thirty diners booked in that day, so we were able to lay up one of the smaller function rooms for the club meeting. Thankfully, breakfast was an easy meal to cater for, but there were still a few minutes of panic behind the scenes in the kitchen. The club members saw none of this, though; they only saw our cheerful, professional attitude and high standard of service, and we didn't have a single complaint.

Eventually, the surprise bookings stopped coming and I was finally able to settle into the running of the hotel.

Quite the gentleman

My friendship with Dennis the bank manager went from strength to strength during his stays at Ragdale Hall. He was a shrewd financier with nostalgia for the exclusive gentlemen's clubs of the past. This nostalgia became a bit of a fantasy for him, and he did what he could to establish a gentlemen's club of his own.

The club wasn't official in terms of being affiliated with one of the existing London clubs or societies, but it was real enough for us. There were only five members, and the rules – such as they were – stated that each of us must contribute something exclusive and beneficial to the other members of the group, and we must never take out more than we put in. The idea was to create mutual opportunities.

Dennis carefully selected the members from among his bank's well-heeled customers and his close friends. Bill Bentley, proprietor of the renowned *Bill Bentley's Oyster Bar*, offered the other members a free night of hospitality at his bar in Swallow Street. The perfect gentleman, Bill was always pleased to see a member of Dennis's club at the bar and treated our ladies like princesses, pulling out all the stops to provide a five-star service. A visit to *Bill Bentley's* never failed to impress the members' dates.

Tom Salter owned several shops in Carnaby Street. He was happy to give large discounts on the latest fashions, along with the occasional freebie. David Moat owned a penthouse in Mayfair which each gentleman had access to, providing it was available. It was a stunning property, and very handy for showing off to friends, investors or dates in London. Dennis, the club's founder and manager, would help members out with any financial problems they encountered, or when they needed advice or a loan.

I was the fifth and last member to be added to this elite gentlemen's club. Of course, I contributed a free weekend at the exclusive Ragdale Hall Hotel to the pot, which my fellow members always seemed to enjoy. It was a strange and wonderful feeling to be invited into this world of perks and favours – another example of the Universe putting me exactly where I needed to be.

The Ghost of Ragdale Hall

Not long after I took over the running of Ragdale Hall, I arranged for a couple of telephone engineers to come and install a modern switchboard. During their break, one of them drew me aside and asked where I came from. When I told him, he asked whether I found life very different out in the country. We had a pleasant enough conversation, but I couldn't help feeling that he was looking for the answer to a question he didn't entirely want to ask.

Eventually, he came to the point and asked me whether I had seen the dog.

I had absolutely no idea what he was talking about. Some hotels keep pets to amuse the guests and keep pests down, but Ragdale Hall didn't have a dog.

"What dog?" I asked him.

"The ghost dog."

That got my attention. I got him and his colleague another cup of tea and invited him to continue.

Apparently, Ragdale Hall was reputed to be haunted by the faithful dog of a former owner. It was a good story, but it didn't wash with me. Ghost animals? It seemed far too fantastical. I asked around when the engineers had gone, and all the local staff members had heard the stories. Some of them even claimed to have seen the dog, but mostly they managed to avoid it as it tended to appear in the dead of night on the top floor of the hotel and in the older parts of the building.

I half forgot the story and got on with the day-to-day business of running the hotel and spa. Then my girlfriend came to stay with me for a while, and one night, she awoke screaming.

"Get the dog off! Get the dog off!"

Just for a moment, I glimpsed it: a big, shaggy dog looking mightily perturbed at having been cast off his comfortable sleeping place. I shot out of bed and switched the light on. If I had been on my own, I would have been utterly terrified, but the fact that my girlfriend was there meant I had to be brave.

I calmed her down and told her that she'd had a bad dream.

I wasn't sure that she believed me, though, and neither of us got much sleep after that.

There was a grand flat on the top floor of Ragdale Hall, commanding spectacular views of the surrounding countryside. Initially, I had planned to move into the flat, so I'd had it furnished and made more homely. I had even moved my things up there, but after hearing about the ghost, I began to wonder whether I would be able to get to sleep in that flat. Instead, I was sleeping in one of the guest bedrooms, which ironically was where I saw the ghost. It didn't seem like a sinister presence, but it was definitely unnerving.

Not wanting a repeat performance of the ghost dog's visit, I moved to a bedroom in the new wing, where I felt much safer. However, the paranormal presence at Ragdale Hall seemed to want my attention. I was sitting up late one evening, reading a book before going to sleep, when I heard noises coming from the ceiling. It sounded like someone was dragging heavy furniture across the floor in the room above – except there was no room above mine. There was only the loft, which was kept locked to prevent drunk guests from getting in and accidentally injuring themselves, or members of the public helping themselves to anything we may have stored up there.

The noises continued every night for a week, but I couldn't bring myself to go up into the loft on my own to check it out. I confess, I was very scared indeed, and I barely slept all week, waiting for the weekend when Jerry would check in and we could investigate the mystery together. I say we, but I was too frightened to go and look. Jerry went up to the loft on his own while I waited anxiously in the hallway below, wanting to be elsewhere.

When he came out of the loft, Jerry looked puzzled, but unafraid. He told me the place was completely empty – there was nothing for anyone to drag and nowhere for anyone to hide. We locked it up again and I tried to put it out of my mind.

That was easier said than done, though, as the dragging noises continued. At first, Jerry didn't believe me, until I challenged him to sleep on the sofa in my room one night.

Both of us were woken by the phantom furniture mover in the small hours of the morning. Jerry leapt from the sofa and hurried up to the loft, ready to surprise whoever was up there (he was convinced it was a member of staff playing tricks on me), but he came back a few minutes later, looking pale and out of sorts. He had found the loft entirely empty as usual, but while he was telling me this, there was a particularly loud thud above our heads. It was as if whatever was up there had been annoyed at Jerry's intrusion.

The paranormal is beyond my control and I don't understand it. I suppose it is an extension of the energies we send out and receive from the Universe during life, but it's all a great mystery to me. And I'm only human – I fear the unknown.

Losing a friend

Time passed and Ragdale Hall prospered. I was happy there, running the hotel, living and working in a house full of history. I had good friends and a good team around me. Everything was going smoothly – or so I thought.

Not everyone was as content as I was. Martin, my hotel manager, was beginning to slip back into his old ways. I think the novelty of the job had worn off and his heart was no longer in it; he was just going through the motions. His lifestyle and the trappings of a managerial position seemed more important to him than his work.

He was okay during the day, but in the evening, Martin would gravitate towards the bar. There, he had his own silver goblet, kept in pride of place, which no one else was allowed to drink from. A table in the restaurant was reserved for him, too – no customers were ever seated there. I think he saw it as one of the perks of his position. From his seat, he could survey the whole room, ostensibly to keep an eye on the smooth running of the service, but the worse his drinking got, the more he treated the staff in the restaurant as his personal servants. He flat out refused to eat staff meals like everyone else, and would order à la carte instead. This was taking up time and resources we couldn't spare.

His issues were turning into a real headache for me. It got to the point where I couldn't close the bar at night because Martin was still there. He would tell me that he'd lock up – and he always did, but he stayed there drinking until the early hours. The late nights inevitably had a negative effect on Martin's ability to do his job properly, though he always looked the part. He would appear at ten in the morning, looking immaculate in a three-piece tailored suit, sporting a freshly picked rose in his buttonhole and a highly polished gold fob watch and chain tucked into the pocket of his waistcoat – Martin had always been a snappy dresser.

Carrying his cigarettes in a gold case which matched his gold Dunhill lighter, he would flash them around to the guests, offering them a smoke and making them feel at home. He loved showing off and always had a tremendous air of confidence about him, like he knew who and what he was and was utterly unashamed of it. Every day, he changed his clothes at least three times in order to keep looking fresh and sharp. I have no idea how he had time to perform his duties between the drink and grooming himself.

It was difficult for me to control Martin because we had been friends for a very long time, and no one enjoys being forced to discipline their good friends. I hated the idea of the two of us falling out, but I suspect he took advantage of my generosity for quite some time at Ragdale Hall.

While I was running the hotel and spa, Jerry and his wife Catherine would visit every weekend, partly to give me moral support (which some days I really needed – running a hotel can be an unforgiving, stressful job at times) and partly to do the books. Jerry had a way with paperwork that was beyond me. The deal was that he would help me balance the books and keep things going along at a steady pace, and I would treat him and Catherine to first class service at Ragdale Hall, wining and dining them in style. They would arrive on the Friday evening and stay for Sunday lunch before returning home to London, and it was an arrangement that suited us all.

Jerry was not a fan of Martin's style of management, and the two of them would often clash. They were complete opposites in terms of personality and outlook, which generally left me in the middle, trying to pick up the pieces and nurse bruised feelings on top of all my other responsibilities. Jerry's self-appointed duties included overseeing the general running of Ragdale Hall, and as Martin's behaviour deteriorated further, he told me that it was no way to run a hotel (or any business).

Martin would have to go.

It was obvious that Jerry was right. Martin was using the hotel to meet his personal needs, rather than him serving the business as the rest of the staff and I did. I agreed that had to change – the hotel and its customers had to come first, but I had no idea how to broach the subject with Martin.

I was still trying to decide how to handle it when events took a turn that forced my hand. One Friday night, I was busy in the disco, transferring the cash from the tills into the secure safe, when Jerry came hurrying over.

"Come quickly," he said, beckoning to me. "You're never going to believe this."

My curiosity was roused, particularly given how Jerry looked – torn between excitement and annoyance. After waiting for me to lock up the safe, Jerry led me upstairs to the first bedroom door on the left. Inside, he pointed to the open window.

I could hear Martin's voice clearly, drifting up from below. His words were rather slurred, but there was no mistaking what he was saying. He was speaking to my head receptionist, a key member of the team at Ragdale Hall, and to my horror, I realised he was trying to persuade her to leave. He was going to quit, he told her, and move to a rival hotel, and he wanted to take her with him.

I was astonished. He was the worse for drink, but I would never have expected Martin – a friend and someone I thought I could trust implicitly – to do something so underhand. The only silver lining to the entire situation was that my head receptionist was having none of it.

I had no choice now – I had to act. It was clear that I couldn't tolerate behaviour like this. Martin was a loose cannon, and now I had evidence of his bad behaviour that he couldn't simply brush off or talk his way out of. Both Jerry and my head receptionist were witnesses to it. Still, though, I was reluctant to let a friend who had been so good to me go.

I was a little relieved, but mostly, I was disappointed. It felt like a double betrayal: I felt like I was betraying Martin by letting him go, while he had betrayed me over and over again by taking advantage of me and the hotel. It was distinctly unpleasant. Looking back over our friendship, I realised that Martin's drinking had been an issue for as long as I had known him – suddenly, I understood why he had never been able to hold down a job.

As the evening wore on, Jerry went to check on the progress of Martin's departure, only to discover that he had made no effort to leave at all. Instead, he was sitting in the bar, drinking heavily with none of his usual light-hearted banter. When he saw me with Jerry, he began shouting abuse at us, muttering dark and evil threats. Any guests who were unlucky enough to be there when we arrived were watching him warily as he spewed venom in our direction, making himself the centre of attention (as he always loved to be) and demanding an audience.

His words scared the hell out of me. Repeatedly, he said he was going to fill his car with petrol and smash it straight through the main entrance of the hotel, killing himself and burning Ragdale Hall to the ground with everyone inside. I hoped against hope that he wasn't serious. He was a bit of a Jekyll and Hyde character; he was the kindest, most generous soul when he was sober, but when the demon drink was upon him, he could become vicious and violent. I seldom saw his darker side, but when I did, it never failed to frighten me.

Eventually, with the help of the larger members of staff, we managed to escort him and his belongings off the property and into a taxi. I watched it drive away, filled with horror at the thought that he might come back to collect his car and act on his awful threat. After he'd departed, I hoped he wasn't intending to stay locally.

I never saw him again.

The awful irony of Martin's departure from Ragdale Hall is that in a way, he predicted his own death. Just over five years after leaving the hotel, Martin was holidaying in Antibes in the South of France with several friends. He and two of his mates were returning home from a raucous night out when the driver pulled over to the hard shoulder, needing to relieve himself. While he was doing his business, a large truck hit the parked car, causing it to explode instantly into an inferno. Martin and the other passenger didn't stand chance; they were both consumed by the flames, burned beyond recognition.

I took Martin's tragic death as a warning, and I want to pass that warning on to you: be careful what you think, say and do. The energy that you release into the world – bad or good – is received by the Universe, and the cosmic forces return it to you in any way they see fit.

All good things come to an end

One of the kitchen porters at Ragdale Hall was a big red-headed Irishman with a fascination for fire – and the occult. When he wasn't on duty in the kitchens, we would often find him burning rubbish in the garden.

At this time, the UK government had just brought in a series of updated fire regulations in the form of a White Paper. Many smaller hotels went out of business because they couldn't afford the new measures, such as keeping an up-to-date fire log, arranging regular inspections from the fire brigade, or installing the new equipment. Luckily, at Ragdale Hall, we were able to stay open, closely monitored by the fire authorities.

My mother came to stay at the hotel for a little while – partly to visit me and partly as a treat. While she was there, she brought the kitchen porter's odd behaviour to my attention. She thought – and I believed her – that he had the potential to be a very dangerous man. Sometimes, I would find our pyromaniac kitchen porter reading the fire leaflets, and I have to admit, it had aroused my suspicions. He had all the makings of a would-be arsonist.

Another of his quirks was that he fancied himself as a bit of a fortune teller – not that he could ever predict anything correctly.

I heard him read for several people, and he got everything wrong each time – they could have got a more accurate reading from a fortune cookie. However, when my mother witnessed him telling fortunes for people (both guests and staff), he was advising them to beware of remaining at Ragdale Hall as it was going to burn to the ground.

This was not long after Martin's traumatic departure, and these 'predictions' disturbed me greatly, particularly given the kitchen porter's predilection for fire. The original Hall that had stood on the site of the hotel had burned to the ground several hundred years ago, killing quite a few people.

The threat of an all-consuming fire began to take over my mind, and before long, the stress became unbearable. I was afraid to leave the building in case my kitchen porter did something stupid or Martin came back to exact his revenge – I was terrified that people would get hurt on my watch and I would have failed them.

I became a prisoner in my own home, locked up in a flammable castle with one enemy in the kitchens and one roaming around God knows where, both ready to strike whenever I wasn't expecting it. My health was suffering, and it was affecting my ability to run the business.

My dream had transformed into a smoke-ridden nightmare.

I am normally a level-headed person, but then I was an emotional wreck. Perhaps my kitchen porter's predictions and Martin's threats were signs sent to warn me to get out while I still could. In the end, I decided that I had to take the difficult and heart-breaking decision to leave the place I loved so dearly.

I put the hotel up for sale and *Slimming Magazine* made an offer. I accepted, and the rest is history.

Leaving Ragdale Hall was an enormous wrench for me. As I drove down the drive for the last time, I was filled with conflicting emotions of relief, sadness and regret. I lamented the chain of events that had made it necessary for me to leave, recalling all the effort it had taken me to purchase the property in the first place. I loved Ragdale Hall; I always will. While I was there, I felt like the Lord of the Manor and I commanded the respect that went with the position. People took me seriously. Sometimes, I think places and people can have a tremendous effect on us. It seems strange to say it, given how short a time I was there in the end, but Ragdale Hall was a big part of my life – and a big part of me.

Good Things Come to Those Who Winnebago

A land yacht with a difference

In 1969, I read an article in one of the Sunday newspapers about the sole importer of American land yachts, which are what we call motor homes here in the UK. They were the ultimate in luxury, equipped with every conceivable extra. The article was a double page spread, and I was so impressed that I displayed it on my office wall, just as I had displayed a picture of my dream car on my bedroom wall on the advice of my grandmother when I was a teenager.

This is a simple and effective means of boosting the impact of your focus. If the thing that you want is buried away among the many other things you think about on a daily basis, your mind cannot focus upon it. However, if the thing you want is on full display – somewhere you will see it every day – the mind will work its magic and the cosmic forces of the Universe will respond with positive energy to influence your decisions and the decisions of those around you, making sure that what you want will be put into your path.

However, I still knew nothing about the Law of Attraction back then; I just knew that focusing on what I wanted had worked for me in the past, and it was to work for me once again.

Four years later, my best friend Mike Quinn and I were at a party on the Kings Road, Chelsea. After leaving the party a little the worse for wear, Mike was driving us home in his red Range Rover. He was stopped by the police and breathalysed, then arrested for driving over the limit. As a passenger, I was not arrested, but the officers allowed me to go along to the police station with him, rather than remain in the middle of nowhere with a vehicle that I was in no state to drive.

Mike was a well-known DJ and television personality in the 1960s and 70s, and while he was in custody, the police were quite proud of their celebrity catch. He was not treated like a common criminal; we were given the five-star treatment, and the police even asked for his autograph. They were fascinated with Mike's showbiz lifestyle.

Mike always enjoyed being the centre of attention, and this occasion was no different. He was so exuberant and cheerful about the whole thing that the officers were charmed by him. During the night, we mentioned Mike's forthcoming tour of Europe and how nice it would be to do it in style in an American land yacht. To our amazement, one of the police officers knew the very man we needed to speak to. This chap's company was just up the road and the officer knew him well, even offering to phone him up on our behalf.

We spent all night in the police station until Mike was sober enough to drive. By then it was 9am on Sunday morning, and Mike and I were stiff and sore, suffering from the usual hangover. The police officer's friend, a larger than life character, arrived and took us to see his selection of Winnebago land yachts. Nothing was too much trouble for him.

Over the next few months, we had a lot of fun partying on

the Winnebago. It was like a magnet – wherever it was parked, it would attract a crowd. Do the same thing today, it wouldn't get a second look. How times have changed.

A close shave in the Alps

The Mike Quinn Show – European Tour kicked off with a vengeance. We were driving from Italy to Denmark, a route which took us over Mont Blanc, the highest mountain in Europe. The shortest distance from A to B went straight through the Great St Bernard Pass, a notoriously dangerous road.

Looking back, I realise it was a foolish route to take. The Winnebago, including the extended bumper and equipment trailer, was 45 feet long. I was driving and Mike was navigating, and we had a roadie with us. After we had been climbing in low gears for some time, negotiating narrow bends and hazardous road conditions, Mike suggested that we turn around and try another route, as this one seemed too dangerous. Unfortunately, it was too late. It was impossible to turn such a vast vehicle around on a narrow road, so we had to keep going and hope for the best.

Eventually, we reached the highest point and the road levelled out. It was still scary because there was a sheer drop on my left hand side, and since the Winnebago was a left-hand drive vehicle, I could see all the way to the valley below. It was rather like I imagine it must feel to fly a plane.

Once we started to descend, the sheer weight of the vehicle had us rapidly gathering speed, which I had little control over. All I could do was keep the Winnebago in a low gear and keep pumping the hydraulic brakes, but it wasn't long before the brakes overheated and stopped working. I started using the handbrake as well, to little effect – I could not slow this monster down. All I could do was to steer the out-of-control machine until it came to rest at the bottom of the pass, hoping not to crash before we reached that point.

I was dreading meeting another vehicle coming the other way – we were travelling fast enough to cause a nasty crash if that had happened. I told Mike to latch the door open so he and the roadie could bail out if they needed to. The last thing I wanted was for anyone to get hurt, but bailing would have to be a last resort as I didn't want to lose my Winnebago, either.

It seemed to take an eternity to cross Great St Bernard Pass. Smoke was pouring in through the open door from the overheated brakes and we were all choking. As each bend approached, Mike and the roadie got ready to jump, but fortunately, they didn't have to. We eventually came to a halt in the village of Martigny in Switzerland.

I have never been so frightened in all my life. Back then, it took two days for me to recover, but now I recognise this event for what it was: another amazing miracle.

A need for speed

My love for Formula One racing never left me. When it was televised, I would make sure I did not miss a race – I would organise my life around the Formula One calendar.

After I returned from the *Mike Quinn Show European Tour*, I had no plans for the future in terms of the Winnebago, so I sent it in to be overhauled and have new brakes fitted. I then stored it away, ready for my next trip.

The Universe had other ideas, though. Not long after the overhaul, my phone rang. To my surprise, it was the March motor racing team, wanting to hire my Winnebago. After a meeting with Rothman's, the main sponsor for the March racing team, I was offered the job of managing the hospitality and catering for the 1976 season. What an opportunity! Ian Scheckter, the brother of Jody Scheckter, the former world champion, was the number one driver for the team, so the Rothman/March partnership clearly had ambitions to succeed in the sport I loved so much. I would have done the job for nothing, but Rothman's paid me a good wage for the privilege of living my dream. I had to pinch myself – was this really happening?

There was a lot of free time between practice sessions, so to stave off boredom, I would spend time socialising with the other teams. On one occasion, I was enjoying a drink in my downtime with Ken

Tyrrell, Founder of Tyrrell Racing, when a young woman approached us. She introduced herself and told us that she was a journalist looking for an interesting story on the racing circuit. Ken and I chatted with her for a while, and then she went on her way. Neither of us thought any more about the meeting with the journalist – after all, the stories we had discussed with her were common knowledge, so we assumed it must have been a fruitless meeting for her.

When I returned to the United Kingdom at the close of the European racing season, my friends couldn't stop teasing me about my time abroad. I had no idea what they were talking about, so I quizzed them further. Finally, one of them produced a copy of a newspaper article written by the young woman Ken and I had spoken to.

Well, it turned out she hadn't been any old hack – she worked for the *News of the World*. After learning nothing of interest from Ken and me, she had simply made up her own story in lieu of the truth – and I'm sure you can imagine the kind of story she made up. What made matters worse was that she had used my name to give credence to her fictitious accounts of the scandalous goings on at the European racing circuit. I have never entirely lived those lies down, and from that day to this, I have never read another newspaper.

As my gran would have said, "You can't believe what you read in the papers."

The deceptive nature of that journalist brought me nothing but irritation. However, it could not detract from the experience of taking part in the racing circuit, and this once-in-a-lifetime experience came about because I had a positive outlook. It was another of many examples of the Law of Attraction doing its good work throughout my life.

The unexplained phenomenon

People who spend a lot of time together can develop an understanding of the minds. This is evident when one of them says what the other is thinking, or finishes the other's sentences, which is often dismissed as coincidence.

It's not.

My father always had a fear of dying alone, so I made him

a promise that this would never happen. I would be with him when the inevitable eventually occurred.

In 1979, I was living in Surrey and my father lived in Dorset. It was not always possible for me to visit him on a regular basis, but I saw him as often as I could.

In November, I received a phone call from my father, asking if I would travel down to Dorset to be with him. I knew exactly what this meant. Needless to say, I cancelled everything and set off, not knowing how long I had to get there. The journey seemed to take for ever – I could not accept that my father was dying. He had always been there for me; he was my rock, my everything. I could not hold back my tears, and I was unable to imagine him not being around any more. All the memories of the lifetime we had spent together came flooding back, and I regretted not having spent more time with him.

He was so pleased to see me when I arrived; it was as if he had been holding on. I tried to put on a brave face for him, but I couldn't stop hugging him. I didn't want him to go.

I was still holding his hand when, after many hours, he slipped into a coma, never to wake again.

When the doctor did his rounds the next day, he said that there was nothing more he could do for my father. The doctor assured me that my father was in no pain and that his time had come.

My dad lingered on for days in the coma. While he was still alive, I spent as much time with him as I could, having catnaps and short breaks here and there. I would talk to him, even though I didn't know if he could hear me or not.

Eventually, though, I had to go back home, telling my father that I would return soon. My son Julian was still a newborn, and I regret to this day that my father never got to meet his grandson before he died. I would phone the hospital every day, but there was no change in his condition.

On the day I was preparing to travel back to Dorset, I experienced my father's presence there with me in Surrey. Phoning the hospital immediately, I knew what I was going to be told, and I was right.

My father had passed away minutes earlier. He had been saying goodbye.

Just in time

New Year's Eve 1983, I was celebrating with friends at the Kings Club, Brighton.

The club was packed to capacity, but to start with, this didn't matter to us at all. We were having such a good night, and the crowds simply added to the party atmosphere. For me, though, the party was about to come to an abrupt end.

As I became separated from my group, losing sight of them in the seething mass of people, I felt an asthma attack coming on. I panicked because I didn't have my inhaler with me, and the panic only served to make my asthma worse. Ordinarily, I wouldn't go anywhere without my inhaler, but I had been distracted by all the excitement of the season. My chest was tightening painfully, and soon I couldn't catch my breath.

I found a bench to sit on and tried to spot my wife among the crowd.

I couldn't see anyone I knew.

I couldn't breathe.

I staggered up the stairs to get out of the club for some fresh air. Trying to hail a taxi, I discovered I could no longer speak. The taxi driver thought I was drunk and refused to take me anywhere.

I slumped to the ground, in serious trouble.

Luckily, a friend of mine, Geoff Draper, came out of the club at that moment and took control. Being as it was New Year's Eve, he knew it would be too late to call an ambulance – they would all be busy by this point, so he shouted at the taxi driver to take us to the hospital as fast as he could. When we arrived, I was rushed into a room and hooked up to various pieces of equipment.

The doctors told Geoff that he did the right thing by not waiting for an ambulance. His quick thinking that night could well have saved my life.

Thank you, Geoff!

An angel in disguise

In 2006, I decided to start up an e-commerce website. I didn't want to get left behind, so I had to bring my business into the twenty-first century to keep up with competition.

With a bit of research, I discovered that many products on the market came from China, and the most popular trade fair was the Canton Trade Fair in Guangzhou. I felt I had to be a part of this trade fair if I wanted to be taken seriously.

After more research, I found out that the Canton Trade Fair was just a few weeks away, and I decided to attend with my good friend, Matthew Coble. We organised the trip as quickly as we could, booking tickets and visas through a travel agent, and within ten days we had everything we needed – even the trade passes we required for the exhibition.

Heading out into Asia for the first time was quite a daunting prospect. Neither of us had ever been before, and we didn't speak Mandarin. We knew that the Chinese culture was very different to the world we knew, and we were worried about accidentally offending people at the trade fair. What we really needed was a guide.

My whole being was focused on China. I would notice Chinese people in crowds, my eyes would be drawn to Chinese restaurants, Chinese writing – anything related to the country. Before this time, I wouldn't have noticed these things at all.

With our tickets and documents prepared, all that was left for me to do was to sell my car in order to fund the trip. I placed an advert in one of the car sales magazines and waited for the phone to ring. Two people expressed an interest in the car, but neither of them bought it. Finally, when I was about to give up hope that anyone would buy my car, the phone rang again. A young lady, Tina, wanted to see it.

Given my interest in all things relating to China, I was astonished to note, when she arrived, that Tina was Chinese. She was very friendly and polite, and when I told her about my impending trip to Guangzhou, she was able to give me a lot of tips and advice about food, culture, places to stay and such in China, which alleviated some of my worries about not being familiar with the country and its customs. She then wished me luck and went on her way.

The following day, Tina called again and asked if she could accompany Matthew and me to China. She told me she was long overdue a trip to see her family back home and she didn't like travelling alone. It seemed like the perfect solution – Tina could help us overcome the language barrier, and we could keep her company and see her safely to her family. She came to my flat to discuss the details of the proposed trip with Matthew and me, giving us a little bit of background on herself. Her name was Tina Tian and she was in the UK to study at Oxford University. She had been married to a Chinese diplomat for several years, but was now divorced. After having met up and got to know each other a bit more, we were all convinced that travelling together would be a great idea.

Matthew and I stayed in Guangzhou for the Canton Trade Fair and Tina went on to Wuhan to see her family. Every day, she telephoned us to make sure we were alright and to find out if we needed anything.

During the week of the fair, I caught a nasty chest infection. Through one of her contacts, Tina arranged for a doctor to come out to visit me at the hotel. He checked me over and provided the proper medication, and within days, I was up and back to normal again. Luckily, the fair ran for two weeks, so I didn't miss out on the experience.

Matthew and I met up with Tina again in Ningbo after the fair. We were there to visit a factory that manufactured some of the products we were interested in, and Tina was a great help, acting as our guide and translator. This made our visit to the factory a lot easier for everyone.

During our stay, we travelled all over China, visiting Beijing, Hangzhou, Chengdu, Shenzhen, Tibet, Hohhot, Shenyang, Nanjing, Shanghai and Hong Kong. It was an extraordinary experience. Everywhere I looked, there was activity. China bustled with life, everyone hard at work making a living for themselves and their families with whatever skills they had. Markets filled with noisy, vibrant stalls sprang up all over the place. People were busy buying and selling, cooking and eating street food, going about their business. In the UK, I was invisible, but in China – which back then attracted fewer tourists – my Western features made me stick out like a sore thumb. Every time we left the house, Matthew, Tina and I would be approached by people wanting to practise their English. I was even asked to give a talk to a class of Chinese children at school. Seeing the Chinese culture and the people's enthusiasm for hard work first-hand, I thought it was no wonder that China is the wealthiest country in the world apart from the USA.

During our stay in China, Tina became a good friend and an extremely useful person to have around. She entered our lives just when we needed her – and when she needed us.

This was the Law of Attraction at work again.

Soulmates

To bring Part I of the book to a close, I would like to share one more experience of the Law of Attraction at work in my life – and this one is a most precious and wonderful example.

During my work with Anthony Robbins, which I will detail in Part II, I was encouraged to write a letter to the powers that be. I then addressed the letter to myself and handed in, and at a date sometime in the future, it would be delivered to me.

Before writing my letter, I was told to focus on my wishes and then write with these wishes in mind. At that time, I had no interest in remarrying. I believed that if I couldn't find the right partner, I was better off alone, but deep down, my dearest wish was to meet my soulmate.

I married my second wife, Lucy, in 2006, and I can safely say that she *is* my soulmate.

Years later, a letter arrived on my doorstep. So much time had passed that I had forgotten all about writing it, and I couldn't believe what I was reading. All those years before, I had asked to meet my soulmate, and I had. I had married her without even realising that my heartfelt wish had come true.

If you think about the thing you want enough, you will surely attract it. I am very glad that I did.

Part II

The Answer

Path to Positivity

The dangers of fear

After all these miracles, why would I need to find the Answer?

There came a time in my life – as there does in many people's lives – when everything seemed to be falling apart. I was unaware of my thinking, and because of the overwhelming nature of the events in my life at the time, I allowed fear to enter my belief system.

Why? How did my belief system change?

I didn't know it at the time, but my luck throughout my life had been based on my thinking. Every time luck came my way, it would reinforce my belief system, and that would empower the next miracle. I was attracting whatever I wanted or needed – the Law of Attraction was in action without me even knowing it.

But when I became afraid, my clarity of thought was compromised, and this, ultimately, was what led to my downfall.

The last few years had been brutal. My wife had seen the writing on the wall and things at home became impossible. Eventually, she left with the children and my marriage of fifteen years broke down. The divorce was messy and the settlement was financially crippling, but the worst of it was being separated from my children. They were still quite young at the time – Clementine, the youngest, was only five and a half – and I couldn't bear the thought of being apart from them, but I no longer had a say in the matter. My wife moved 300 miles away, taking the children with her.

I remember the first time I came home to a completely empty house. I walked through every room, trying to hold on to the memories of my children sleeping, growing, playing there; the memory of when my wife and I had first moved in. We had been so happy, and the house had seemed homely and bright. Now it was overwhelmingly quiet and still, as if its heart had been torn away along with mine. In a way, I suppose it had.

Over the next few years, I watched my life fall apart. Poor business decisions and mismanagement on my accountant's part crippled me financially. Interest on my loans had risen to 15% and I was struggling to keep up my repayments. I'd been selling off my hotels to cover costs, but there always seemed to be something else that needed to be paid for. I threw myself into work, desperately trying to salvage what I could.

It was at the very depths of my despair that the tax office declared me bankrupt and the bailiffs moved in.

I got caught out by the capital gains tax law. Because the price I got for every hotel I sold was taxed at 40%, whether or not I replaced the hotel or had higher outgoings than before, I ended up with an extortionate tax bill that I had no way of paying. My accountant could have advised me to form a limited company, which would have ensured that my home, car, private possessions and Spanish villa would have remained separate from my business interests, but he didn't. Because my company wasn't limited, when I was declared bankrupt, it affected all my assets, not just my business. The Inland Revenue took me to pieces.

The receivers took everything of value – that is, everything that could be sold to help pay off my debt. They let me keep goods that had no saleable value, like family photographs, and took everything else. The three bailiffs who came into my house were thugs and bullies. At one of the hardest times in my life, they showed no mercy or compassion, leaving me with what they deemed to be the barest necessities. When they had finally gone, the only things I had left were the clothes on my back.

The only good thing about this episode was that I no longer owed the bank any money and my only creditor was the Inland Revenue.

I was at the lowest point in my life when my son, Julian, came to visit me. I had lost everything – my business, my home, my possessions, my family – so needless to say, I was not in a good place. I had no self-respect; I felt that I had nothing left to give. I was a shadow of the man I had been – the father he remembered.

It was his kindness, however, that gave me the courage to begin the process of recovery. He had heard of a man named Anthony Robbins – an American guru who ran a highly successful self-help programme. But by this point, of course, I had very little money, barely enough to live day-to-day. How was I going to afford an expensive self-help programme?

My wonderful son offered to take care of everything. He could see that I needed help, and he reached out to me. The trip was organised in a matter of weeks.

I couldn't believe it.

As my plane left London for Hawaii, I began to feel hope for the first time in years.

Letting go of my negativity

The Anthony Robbins course took place in two parts, the first being in Hawaii and the second in Miami. Many of my fellow students had also reached rock bottom. Each of us began the course having encountered hurdle after hurdle, believing that everything was against us. Between us, we had very little hope left.

Anthony was a fantastic host. He was so full of energy – in no time at all, he had us doing things we never thought we could. His zest for life was infectious.

The first part of the course was an intensive ten-day positivity boot camp. It was a refreshing way to live, even for only a few days. From ten o'clock in the morning until past midnight, we threw ourselves into activities such as fire-walking and trapeze work. We faced our fears head-on, and were so exhausted by the end of every day that we no longer had time to dwell on our problems.

The course progressed at a rapid pace, and I found myself wondering, in the peace of each morning, what impact it would have on my life, my future. My negativity, which I had held on to for so long, was gradually falling away. It was replaced not with positivity just then, but with the knowledge that I could do extraordinary things.

Every day, Anthony would ask us whether we felt we had made a breakthrough, and each day a few more members of the group would raise their hands to indicate that yes, they had. At first, I didn't understand what he meant. What was a 'breakthrough'? What did it mean on a personal level? How would I know if I'd had one? I wondered what it would feel like – would it be my means of getting on with my life? Would I have a future worth fighting for?

I left the boot camp in Hawaii feeling liberated, refreshed and emotionally recharged. The experience had freed me from the negativity which had been hanging over me like a cloud, fogging up my thoughts and obscuring my path. My subconscious had been ruling my life, pushing me towards the wrong attitudes and decisions in a downward spiral of self-fulfilling prophecies. How long had I been living like this? It was time for a change.

Getting back on my feet

I arrived in Miami ready for whatever the second part of the course would throw at me. This time, rather than facing our fears, we were encouraged to develop tools for coping with everyday life, building on our new-found positivity to take us closer to our personal goals.

It was a week of revelations. For the first time, we had the time to reflect on the way we had chosen to live – not to dwell on past mistakes or wallow in self-pity, but to learn from our choices; to make use of them. Slowly, we were learning together to build a plan of action to carry us forward.

For years, I had been living in a kind of spiritual bubble, inadvertently shielding myself from positivity and opportunity. I had been making the same mistakes as many other people, allowing myself to become subjected to negative influences from modern media: television, advertising, social networks, sceptics, and the eternal droning of the press. I had been focusing all my energy on the things these media wanted me to believe were important in life: wealth, status, and a media-led idea of beauty and possessions.

In the 1980s, I thought I had it all: a beautiful wife; four incredible children; a successful chain of hotels and restaurants. My wife and I even had domestic staff catering to our every whim. I put my children through expensive private schools, trying to give them the best start in life, forgetting that the best start I could possibly give them was spending time with them. I kept and raced a pedigree horse, and my wife would travel the length of the UK, attending race meetings. We entertained our friends frequently. I could afford the best, so I bought the best.

Over time, work began to consume me. Before, I had been driven by the will to succeed, but then I started putting myself under tremendous pressure to maintain the extravagant lifestyle to which my family had become accustomed. I was working late more often than dining with my family, and between work, school and our social lives, I barely saw them. My wife and I became strangers in the same house. Holidays and quality time became a thing of the past – once, I worked instead of going on a planned family holiday, sending the domestic staff along in my place. I was so busy making money, I couldn't see how much it was costing me personally.

Although many of my choices were flawed, I had to accept that some things were not my fault. The Greek philosopher Epictetus once wrote:

> Of all existing things some are in our power, and others are not in our power.

This is as true today as it was in ancient Greece.

During my week in Miami, I came to a point where I was ready to let go of *all* my negativity – not just my bitterness at the way things had turned out, but also the conviction that all my misfortunes were my fault. Some things were simply beyond my control.

The breakthrough

I was breakfasting alfresco when it hit me.

I had chosen to eat alone that morning, enjoying the peace and quiet before the day's revitalising session. The sun was shining; birds were flocking above the sparkling North Pacific; waves rolled and crashed lazily against the golden sand. Below me on the beach, a group of people were doing their morning workout, roller-skaters whizzing past them despite the early hour. As I watched and listened, breathing in the sea air, I allowed myself simply to *be*. I found myself at peace.

A tremendous sense of calm washed over me, like the waves were washing on to the beach below. I felt lighter – enlightened. It was as if I had opened my heart to the world for the very first time, and the world had given me back something of indescribable beauty. It filled me up, like a lantern fills a dark room with golden light. I let the all the stress, the bitterness, and the self-recrimination of the past few years fall away. Finally, guiltlessly, I relaxed.

In that moment, I felt such utter peace and clarity, it was as if I had been transported to another plane of consciousness. I felt alive and aware for the first time. It was a spiritual awakening.

Later that same day, when Anthony asked the group whether anyone had had a breakthrough, I raised my hand with the rest. I was ready to move on with my life; I had remembered what it was to be alive. It was an extraordinary life-changing emotion that I would love to be able to tap into at any time.

During our final days in Miami, Anthony asked us to write a letter to the powers that be – the letter I mentioned at the end of Part I – and address it to ourselves. We each wrote down the thing we wanted most in the world – a wish, if you will – sealed the letters and handed them in. I forgot about my letter for a long time, but when it did arrive, I realised that my wish had most definitely come true.

I would love the same thing to happen to you, whatever your circumstances, whatever your deepest wishes.

The Law of Attraction

Throughout this book, I refer to a system of belief known as the Law of Attraction. If you're getting a little confused, then this section is for you.

The Law of Attraction is one of nature's 'laws', like gravity, the steady movement of time and the way buses seem to come in threes. Based on the theory that like attracts like, the Law of Attraction means that whatever you think, you attract. People who look at the world in a negative way will naturally draw negativity towards themselves. Similarly, people with an optimistic outlook will naturally draw positivity towards themselves.

This is not to say that the bad things which happen to us are our fault. We live in a world made up of a great number of people who are all focusing their thoughts on a great many things. Sometimes, the things that others want have an impact on our lives, and sometimes, sadly, bad things just happen. Friends move away; relationships break down; family members are injured or pass away. Sometimes breaking a plate really is an accident. Don't come to believe you are somehow cursing yourself with negativity when things happen that are out of your control. Even the most positive person can go through a hard time – it's what you choose to make of negative events that impacts your life.

If you think that bad things are always happening to you, you will become negative, thus attracting more negative influences and events. If, however, you accept that bad things can happen to anyone and are optimistic about the future, then you will attract more positive influences and events. In effect, you can create your own turning point.

This is the Law of Attraction at work.

Consider the saying, "Be careful what you think." Your thoughts are vibrations in the ether that emanate from within you. They interact with everything and everyone around you, and most importantly, they send your 'wishes' to the Universe.

It is human nature to doubt what you cannot see and dismiss things that you don't understand or don't feel comfortable with. At times, it may feel like every monkey and his uncle has a new belief that they promise will revolutionise your life. Don't listen to them.

Take the time to evaluate the Law of Attraction and the power it can have in your life. It has manifold advantages and absolutely no risks. Put aside your scepticism and give the Law of Attraction a chance. What have you got to lose? The Law of Attraction has worked for me and for thousands of others.

Trust in the Universe

Though you cannot see radio waves being transmitted through the air, modern communication continues daily without any perceivable problem. Similarly, just because you cannot perceive your thoughts – or those of others – travelling through the ether to the Universe, it does not mean that they aren't there, or that they can't influence your life.

We all live in parallel with the metaphysical dimension, and this is the source we need to tap into in order to make our connection with the Universe more solid. Throughout our lives, we create the person we are. We have spent every moment from birth unconsciously moulding the person we are today. I don't mean this in terms of what we wear, or what we eat, or how we choose to style our hair; I'm talking about changes we have made on a deeper plane. With our thought vibrations, we each shape our very existence, attracting things to us and changing who we become.

You have the power to alter your own reality, to mould the world in which you want to live, simply by changing the way you think. We are all who we choose to be. Take responsibility for your choices, and accept the consequences. Now that you are aware of the Law of Attraction, take control of your thoughts to attract a better life for yourself. You can create a new reality – it is within your power to do so.

The process of the Law of Attraction begins in our own brains and can be activated through the practice of meditation, focusing on your goals and desires. You can easily recognise when to utilise this power – when you first encounter a wish or desire, you will feel a rush of excitement, strengthened by the desire. This is the time to take action. The Law of Attraction will not work unless you take action. If you don't act upon your desire immediately, the good vibration will lose its power.

"What you think, you become."

The Buddha

It's not the job of the Universe to make things happen in your life – you have to work towards them. You provide the inspiration – dream it, allow yourself to believe, and help the Universe to bring it into being. The spark, the catalyst – that's for the Universe to provide. The Law of Attraction will make it happen.

Once I had welcomed the Law of Attraction into my life and had accepted the enormous advantages that lay ahead of me, it became second nature for me to tune into the cosmic forces and meet them halfway. I became a better, more open person; I was more aware of my actions and their impact on others. I was in tune with my mind, body and soul – my whole being was in harmony.

The art of expectation

In your faith, your joy, you conceive the path to your own goals and happiness. If you maintain your belief, prolonging your vibrational harmony with the cosmic forces, the Universe will find a way to make your goals happen. The Universe cannot help you achieve your dreams if you can't maintain a consistent level of communication.

It is difficult to maintain that level of intensity over the weeks or months you may need to wait for the Universe to fulfil your wish, so you need to cultivate your expectation. Feel the same excitement that a small child feels before an important event in their lives, such as their birthday or on Christmas Eve. Remember that impatience is not the same thing as expectation. Expectation is a positive feeling that emphasises the message you are hoping to convey, while impatience can conflict with your message. Prevent your expectation becoming impatience.

How many times in your life have you needed something to happen, and lo and behold, happen it has – but not in the way you expected? The Universe identifies your desire through the direction and intensity of your vibrations, and provides it in any way it sees fit. You may be focusing on wealth and thinking that it will appear in the form of a sudden windfall or lottery win, but the Universe doesn't necessarily think like that. Instead, you may receive an unexpected pay rise; a more lucrative job offer; an inheritance; an opportunity to sell an old car. Rather than being careful what you wish for, perhaps you would be better off being careful how you wish for it. Be specific. If you want the money for a new car, focus your energy on the car instead of the wealth. If you want a new house, the perfect wedding, a trip to Jamaica – whatever, focus your desire on those things rather than the money itself.

Money comes and money goes; experiences and memories

are far more precious. It's possible that the Universe will find an unexpected way of fulfilling your wishes. For example, if your desire is for a holiday abroad, you may be offered accommodation free in return for keeping an eye on the place you are staying. If transportation is an issue, perhaps a friend who is scared of flying will be going to the very place you want to visit and will offer to pay for your flight in return for your moral support. Maybe you'll be offered a job in your dream holiday location, giving you ample opportunity to explore the area in your time off.

Say that one of your deepest wishes is to write a novel, but you never seem to have the time. Imagine that you focus all your energy on having the opportunity to write your book and the inspiration and commitment to finish it. You may then come across something that interests or appeals to you, perhaps in your daily life, perhaps in a book or film. The fact that you have encountered this inspiration at a time in your life when you are ready to write your book will be no accident; the Universe will have found a way to introduce the first element you need into your life. If you have made yourself receptive to the Universe, the idea will grow in your mind.

It takes a very centred person to believe that they will succeed at a venture, particularly one as personal as writing a novel. This is where you meet the Universe halfway and let the Law of Attraction bring inspiration and opportunity into your life. Once you have taken the plunge and started writing, you may find that there are not enough hours in the day to get things done. Perhaps you have a busy day job or a demanding family life. If you focus on having more time to concentrate on your writing, the Universe will help you to succeed. It may help you rearrange or reschedule your daily routine to give you the time you need, or it may do something more drastic. You wouldn't tend to regard something like losing your job as a positive thing, but it may happen just when you want to focus on a creative project like writing your book. Losing a job may be the Universe's way of allowing you the time you need to sit and write.

Sometimes the things that seem negative and difficult to deal with have the most positive impact in your life. Trust in the Universe – it will take care of you. Everything happens for a reason.

This is particularly important to remember if you are wishing for a soulmate. In this case, it's easy to get drawn into thinking about what you *don't* want in a significant other, which will send the wrong message out to the Universe. It can't tell the difference between the things you do and don't want; all it can tell is that you are focusing on a particular thing with great intensity. And that's the thing that will be attracted to you, whether you want it or not.

If it helps you to keep track of what you are focusing your energy on, make a list of the traits or aspects that you do want in your soulmate. Cut out images from magazines of things that symbolise what you want: a ring for commitment; clasped hands for friendship; a flower for delicacy. Whatever the image, make sure it speaks to you about that particular trait.

A useful modern tool for this exercise is Pinterest. On this website, you can create boards of specific images which can be either kept private or shared with the wider social media community. You may dedicate a board to the car of your dreams, or how you want your garden to look, and it can then be used when you meditate to help you focus on your desires every day. While you are collating your images, you will be focused entirely on what you want – this, too, will help to transmit your positive vibrations to the Universe.

Remember, if you don't believe in the power of the Universe and the Law of Attraction, then it will never work for you. Remove all doubt from your mind and focus your being on achieving pure and meaningful communication with the Universe. There are many different names for this communication: some call it prayer, or magic, or affirmations, or manifestation. Whatever you call it, pour your heart and soul into your request. The more effort you put into your desire, the more likely it is to be fulfilled.

Don't, whatever you do, lower your expectations. You deserve to be happy, and you deserve to have the opportunities in life that will enhance your soul's journey. Never underestimate yourself, or your power to change your life for the better.

Cosmic ordering

Cosmic ordering is another way to describe the process of the Law of Attraction, though it is a more simplified view. This splits the process into three phases: requesting (or manifesting), belief (or faith), and receiving (or accepting).

Simply put, the requesting phase describes the way we decide on what it is we want and then transmit our positive vibrations to the Universe. We need to sit down and consider carefully what it is that we particularly want or need. Our minds are often so busy and full of clutter that we can barely tell what it is, so it is important to meditate and clear our minds before preparing to transmit our vibrations. The Universe needs clarity.

In order for the Universe to act on the desires and wishes you transmit to it, develop and maintain faith in the Universe and in yourself. There's no point in asking the Universe to help you with something if you don't love and respect yourself. If you only consider yourself in terms of what you've done or are doing 'wrong', what is 'wrong' in your life, and what is 'wrong' with you, then your clear, well-thought-out desires will get confused and perverted.

It is easy to get caught up in the modern-day culture of blame and self-hate, particularly when we are constantly bombarded by media representations of what we should have, what we should look like, what we should do, but try not to get side-tracked. A good credo to live by is this: if it's not hurting anybody (including you), then no one should have a problem with it. If other people *still* profess to have a problem with it, then it's not you who has the problem. It is an aspect of *their* negativity that they are trying to project on to you. Ignoring these negative influences is easier said than done, but do your best. No one can ever ask any more of you than that.

If you have faith in yourself then you will find it much easier to put your faith in the generosity and efficacy of the Universe. Truly believe that a thing will come to you, and it will appear. It may not materialise in the way you expected – there are manifold ways that the Law of Attraction can bring things into your path – but it *will* appear.

This is not to say, of course, that you can just ask for something without doing any of the work yourself. You have to meet the Universe halfway. A good example of this is when I was trying to secure the purchase of Ragdale Hall, and the subsequent struggles I went through to keep it functioning. Despite the machinations of others, I managed to pull off the impossible. I put every effort into it and was able to reap the rewards. I never even entertained the possibility of giving up – if I had, all would have been lost. I believed in myself, and forces that were at the time beyond my knowledge and control made sure I succeeded.

The third phase is the fun part: getting what you want. When the Universe fulfils your desires – possibly not in the way you imagined – accept what you asked for, and be grateful. Appreciate the glorious gift the Universe has given to you.

First Steps

The hardest part

The first and most important step you can take towards turning your life around is to decide that you want it to happen. Know in yourself that you are prepared to work for your happiness. Give yourself permission to change.

Admitting that you need a helping hand to change is one of the most difficult things anyone can do. Congratulations – by picking up this book you have made a subconscious decision to change. Now all you need to do is allow your conscious self to take the same leap.

In my case, I had to take a hard look at myself to see where I was going wrong. It was a decision of the utmost importance – it would change my life. I had to be brave. Desperately wanting to change, I had to start immediately. I took a step outside my comfort zone and faced the challenges and obstacles in my path head on.

As my gran would have said, "No pain, no gain."

With all the knowledge I gained from the Anthony Robins seminars, I was ready. Nothing was going to stand in my way, if I could only muster the courage to act. It was time to put a stop to the procrastination that was holding me back. I knew that it wasn't going to be an easy ride, but nothing worthwhile ever is.

I asked myself what would happen to me if I didn't choose to make a change right then and there. Where would I be in one year's time? Five years? Ten years? It was too terrifying to imagine.

Negativity weighs you down. If you carry it around with you, it prevents you from reaching your full potential. Moreover, it prevents you from receiving all the opportunities the Universe has in store for you. Remember Epictetus? Some things will always be beyond your control.

Let them go.

Reflect on the past

There may have been times in your life when you've asked yourself, "How did I get here? How can this have happened to me?" The likelihood is that the answers are more obvious than you think.

The Universe is constantly sending you opportunities, but if you aren't in tune with the Universe, the chances are you won't recognise these opportunities. Find your centre, clear your mind and listen – the Universe will provide. Look back over the events that have shaped your life so far. The Universe has always been on your side.

When I look back at my life, I can see many examples of the Law of Attraction working for me, a number of which I have shared in Part I. The powers that be work in mysterious ways. For example, the Universe arranged things so that Tina – a native Mandarin speaker who had grown up with the customs and cultures of China and wished to visit her homeland – picked up the particular paper that contained the advert I'd placed when I was selling my car. At this time, the one thing I needed more than anything was a guide in China. Out of the blue, her path and mine crossed just at the right time. We could have simply said goodbye and never seen each other again, but instead, we grabbed the opportunity that the Universe had laid in front of us, and it worked out wonderfully for both of us.

Taking stock

There comes a time in everyone's life when we need to pause, get off the relentless treadmill of routine, and take stock.

Set aside a little time and ask yourself a few questions. You may find it helps to record your thoughts with a pen and paper, or on your phone or computer. Whatever method you decide on, though, it is important to do this at a time when you are relaxed and free from distractions.

Ask yourself:

- What have I achieved in my life?
- Is this what I really want?
- Am I happy?
- What can I do to improve my life, situation and/or happiness?

Give these questions some serious and honest thought, and then write down your answers. It may be that some answers will be unpalatable to you, but don't mentally edit or amend them in any way. If you can't be honest with yourself, then the bounty of the Universe will never come to you.

There are many difficult times in life where people are tempted to apportion blame. Perhaps you are under financial strain; perhaps you are going through a messy divorce; perhaps you have lost someone dear to you. Fear, anger and desperation can set in, but don't let them take over your life. Trust in the Universe, have faith in yourself, and the Law of Attraction will help you on your way to getting your life back to where you want it to be.

In the case of a divorce, either party – especially the injured party – may fear that time is running out for them. For women who want to have children, the ticking of the biological clock can be particularly unnerving. They only have a limited time to be with the people they love, find that perfect partner, start a family. A combination of fear and desperation may push them into thinking that they don't have time to find the person who is right for them. They may experience an extraordinary fear of being alone.

For me, the fear of ending up homeless, like my awful experience in Liverpool in my youth, drove me to work myself into the ground to maintain a certain standard of living. In the end, though, the negativity that I had inadvertently allowed to rule my life robbed me of everything I held dear. I had turned my back on the opportunities the Universe had for me, and it very nearly destroyed me.

Do not listen to negative thoughts. You are the most important thing in your life. Do not allow yourself to be caught up in fear or anger associated with your situation; it will only drive you to waste the time you have on this earth. Every day is a gift – enjoy it; take full advantage of your time. The likelihood is you will be pleasantly surprised.

Choose your path through life for the right reasons. Almost everything we do in life is geared towards the pursuit of happiness, but often that happiness is fleeting and superficial. There may have been times when you just *had* to have one more glass of wine; one more slice of cake; play one more game on your console, but beware of over-indulgence. All these things can contribute to a happy and healthy life, but only in moderation. Drugs and alcohol in particular can give you an illusion of happiness, but it's not real. Overused and abused, they will bring you nothing but misery. Everything you do or do not do in your life will have an impact on your future.

In truth, you deserve more than a fleeting form of happiness – and so do your family and friends. The smallest of adjustments to your plans and goals will have an enormous effect on the outcome of your life journey. Instead of allowing yourself to be seduced by the media into letting corporations take all of your hard-earned money, you will be able to save, focusing your energy and resources on achieving the life you want to live. You don't have to buy into something to be happy; you don't need the lifestyle the media is trying to sell to you – you need what works for you. Your money is far better off in your bank account, and your time and energy are better invested in your life and happiness.

> Don't feel stupid if you don't like what everyone else pretends to love.
>
> Emma Watson, actress and inspirational speaker

There are many pleasures to be had in life without turning to drugs, alcohol or spending money. Focus on these simple pleasures and they will have a positive impact on the quality of your life.

Outdoor pursuits such as fishing can have a calming effect and can get you in tune with nature. You may find gardening particularly rewarding as your efforts will have a tangible result. Sports such as golf, football, rugby, swimming, cycling, roller derby – whatever you most enjoy doing – are great for your health. You can burn off excess energy, keep in shape and socialise with friends on a regular no-pressure basis.

Indoor pursuits could include joining a choir or singing group. Singing can really boost your confidence and provides another opportunity to meet new friends. If you prefer solitude, then learning to make things can be a rewarding pursuit – and help you to save money. You could pick up some new skills at your local college or university. Many of these institutions have low cost and occasionally free courses covering a wide range of subjects, from modern languages and gardening to cake decorating to IT skills, which can also help you in your career or home life.

There are few more rewarding experiences than helping others. Could you spare your time to help out in your local hospice, or visit your local primary school and help young children to gain confidence in their reading? If you love to cook or garden, perhaps you could share your produce with a local goodwill café or community garden.

There is a wide range of opportunities out there if you are willing to give up a little of your time and energy to help others. The rewards may not be tangible, but giving is a wonderful balm for the soul.

Find your inspiration

The first step in gaining the knowledge and tools that you need to let the Universe in is to read the right kind of books, listen to the right kind of talks and watch the right kind of films.

A book that certainly helped me understand how I could work in harmony and communicate with the Universe is the bestselling *Think and Grow Rich* by Napoleon Hill. This book inspired me, lighting the fire and imbuing me with the burning desire that I need to succeed. It's a great resource and I absolutely recommend it.

Forgive

You can never be in a peaceful, centred state if you cannot learn to forgive others. This is more difficult than it sounds and it's a skill that can take a long time to master.

Let go of any grudges. Resentment or anger does nothing except hurt you and the people around you. It rides your back like a goblin, turning your head and whispering venom into your ear. Learning to forgive is an important step on the path to positivity, but it sometimes seems like the very last thing in the world you will ever be able to do. Don't just do it for those you need to forgive, do it for yourself.

The most important person you need to forgive is yourself. If you cannot forgive yourself, the Law of Attraction just won't work. Have compassion – ask yourself what you would say to a friend if they came to you for advice having made the same mistakes as you have.

Remember that your choices – and those of others – are half chance. Sometimes, you are forced into making decisions by circumstance. A mistake can stay with you for years, eating away at you through embarrassment, anger, and fear.

Let all that resentment and fear go. Take a deep breath and do it.

Ask for forgiveness

When you feel that you are ready, ask the Universe to forgive you. This isn't about sins or broken taboos, but about the mistakes that have come to define you – the mistakes that have made you a prisoner of your own past.

Ask for forgiveness for being unable to see the wonders of the Universe; for being unable to recognise the beauty all around you; for ignoring the opportunities in your life. Remember, every mistake we have ever made is an opportunity to learn. Mistakes, therefore, are also sent to us by the Universe. Make your peace with your mistakes and use them to grow.

Everyone wants forgiveness for something, however minor a transgression it may seem. It could be for something as simple as being impatient and accidentally knocking into someone, or having a lack of understanding of a situation and causing discomfort or injury to someone through misinterpretation.

You need to create a direct line to the cosmic forces that govern all our lives, and to achieve that, you need to unblock your energy channels. Bearing in mind we are discussing things on a metaphysical level here, the first blockages to address are spiritual and emotional, and forgiveness is a major unblocking technique. Forgive others and ask for their forgiveness – and be prepared to accept that you are worthy of that forgiveness.

Harmony and communication with the Universe

In order to communicate with the Universe on a metaphysical level, first learn to clear your mind of all your worries, fears and regrets. This is easier said than done, so don't feel daunted if your head is too full right now. This isn't the kind of thing you can pick up straight away – it takes time.

Personal harmony is difficult to define. Some see it as inner peace; some as everything just feeling right; some as moving effortlessly through the crowd. However you experience it, personal harmony is good for the heart and the soul.

Take a deep breath and let go of everything that's in your head, stopping you from communicating with the Universe. Listen to the sounds of the world around you. The Universe is always telling you something. All you need to do is listen.

Take action to avoid procrastination

Even with the best intentions and the most rigorous planning, you will find your mind wandering. The trick is to avoid falling into a procrastination trap.

Procrastination will take on different forms depending on who you are. If you enjoy computer games, you may decide to play 'just ten more minutes'; if reading is your thing, you may decide to read 'just one chapter' of your book. You may spend hours planning exactly what you intend to achieve in a day and then decide you absolutely *have* to clean the entire house before you get started.

In terms of procrastination, often our worst enemy is ourselves. In my case, I put off things I didn't want to do, or that felt daunting to me, until the next day – and then the next day, and the next. Eventually, even the thought of attempting tasks that had once been commonplace made me panic and caused me anguish. Of course, it then became a vicious circle: the more I panicked, the more I avoided the tasks; the more I avoided the tasks, the more I panicked at the mere idea of them. In the end, I found myself avoiding tasks – often tasks that should have been easy to achieve – for as long as possible.

That said, don't forget to take regular breaks. Taking a break isn't the same as procrastination; sometimes your brain needs to do something different. Try to intersperse energetic activities with quieter ones, and sedentary or academic activities with energetic ones. Sit and read quietly for five minutes; do the dishes; stick the radio on and dance to your favourite song; plan what you're going to have for dinner – do whatever you need to do to give yourself a rest.

Most importantly, don't feel guilty if you haven't done the million and one things you felt you absolutely had to finish today. Life does not always work that way. Enjoy the days when it does, and learn to appreciate where the Universe is taking you on the days when it doesn't.

Have faith

Don't underestimate yourself. You are a remarkable, valuable person. There is only one of you, anywhere. There will only ever be one of you, through all of time. Cherish the things that make you 'you': all your idiosyncrasies; the songs you love; the food you love; the stories you tell; the things that make you laugh, cry, smile. The Universe would be a smaller and less interesting place without you in it.

So what if you don't fit in with what society tells you is desirable? It's not up to society; it's up to you. You can make a difference, even if it seems like a small thing. That 'one small thing' can move mountains, so celebrate your achievements – even if it seems daft. You are worth celebrating.

Many of the challenges we face in life seem, at first, to be impossible to overcome, but often it's our own attitude that's holding us back. The Universe never gives us more than we can handle, even though it may occasionally seem like it.

Fear is a debilitating emotion. It can take over every aspect of your life, affecting your health, preventing you from performing your daily routine and stopping you from enjoying life. It can even be a killer. Never underestimate the power of fear.

Nine times out of ten, though, things aren't nearly as terrifying as they first appear. Much of the time, we allow our negative beliefs, built up over a lifetime of experience, to block our energy channels.

Have you ever wondered why young children seem so carefree? It is because they have not yet encountered all the things that could possibly go wrong in any given situation. Where an adult will have an internal script detailing myriad possibilities for failure, children only have the vision of what they would like to achieve.

Unblock your energy channels, let go of your old belief system and make way for the new one: anything is possible when you put your mind to it. The Universe is vast and unending – a place of infinite wonder and possibility. There is a place for every person within it. Find your place. Have faith in yourself, and the Universe will provide. The Universe wants you to succeed – the only thing standing in your way is you.

Take a little advice from American poet and photographer, Tyler Knott Gregson:

> I cannot fathom
> How tall your trees
> Could grow
> If you stopped
> Chopping the tops
> In fear of someone else
> Cutting you down.

Develop a positive outlook

It may sound obvious, but you need to maintain a positive outlook before you can access the power of the Universe. It's no good trying to manifest something positive if your outlook or focus is entirely negative.

For example, say you want a new job. Don't focus your thoughts or energy on how much you hate your present role, or how many times you've been turned down by potential employers (or never heard anything back from them) in the past. The Universe can't differentiate between a positive and negative thought. The more you focus on the bad time you're having at work, the more the Universe will pick up on it, sending even more frustration your way because frustration is precisely what you are focusing on.

Let go of negative energy. Take a look at yourself in the mirror and focus on the good things that you want to manifest. Instead of saying, "I hate my job, I wish I could get another", say, "I will get a new job and it's going to be awesome." It's difficult to evade negative thoughts sometimes (don't worry, we all have bad days), but try to put your frustration aside when you are focusing on what you want to manifest.

Foster excitement

Gifts from the Universe are not instant – although sometimes it may seem like they are. Like a storm over the sea or the first blush of blossom on a cherry tree in spring, the gifts are not single instances but long processes built up over time. Don't get upset if your wish does not arrive straight away – it will come to you when you are ready, so keep faith in the process. Good things really do come to those who wait.

Did you ever stay awake all night on Christmas Eve to catch a glimpse of Santa Claus? How about counting down the days to your birthday, or your wedding day? This is the kind of focused energy that the Universe will sit up and pay attention to.

Once you have made your wish, *know* that it will come true, deep down inside. Don't listen to rational adult arguments that will get in the way, telling you how difficult your wish will be to achieve. Everything can be difficult, but that doesn't make it impossible. Nothing is impossible. Focus your energy on what you really want to achieve, and you *will* get there.

Human beings are a remarkable species. We are curious, determined, magnificent. As a group and as individuals, we find ourselves making new discoveries, reaching new heights and achieving what we previously imagined to be impossible. Every generation of humanity stretches the boundaries of possibility – if we showed our modern advancements to people two generations ago, they wouldn't believe their eyes.

Think about the development of technology in the twentieth century, for example. In 1900, the idea of humans flying through the air in anything other than a hot-air balloon was ridiculed. Eleven years later, the first successful flight took place – and fifty years after that, humans were in space. Ten years after the first manned space mission, we were landing on the moon. In less than a century, we had turned flying from impossible into something we do on a regular basis.

I do most of my writing at night. Sometimes, as with all endeavours of a creative nature, I hit a brick wall in my work. Writer's block is a common curse, draining energy and inspiration. When I reach that point, that is the time I must go to sleep, no matter how much or how little I have got done, or wanted to achieve. On these occasions, I tune my mind to the problem at hand, as I would if I were intending to meditate (we will discuss meditation in the next chapter). Every time, without fail, my mind has found the answer I was seeking by morning.

There is no point pushing yourself to the point where you burn out. Learn to take care of yourself.

As humans, our curiosity and tenacity allows us to delve into the wonder of the Universe – but we seldom use it to discover ourselves. Be excited about the gifts you are going to receive, whenever they will be. Foster the same kind of excitement you felt about Santa, or your birthday, or your wedding – the restless, happy, fizzing kind of excitement that lives inside your skin and gets you moving in the morning. Smile more – it's good for you. Not only will excitement allow the Universe to help you fulfil your goals, you will be genuinely happy.

Essential Tools and Techniques

Unblocking techniques

In order to listen to the Universe, first learn to unblock your mind. Think of this as a form of mental and spiritual detoxification.

Whatever you think you are is what you will become. If you think of yourself as unsuccessful, cowardly, overweight, unhappy or unlucky, then you will become those things. If, however, you give yourself permission to think of yourself as successful, courageous, slim, happy or lucky, then these are the things that you will be. Our thoughts personify us, so take care what you think of yourself.

If you want to be a dancer, then dance. If you want to be a writer, then write. If you want to be the best at crown green bowling, then bowl. If you want to be a world-class zoologist, then practise zoology. Of course, you won't wake up tomorrow and suddenly be a world-class zoologist, but you will be closer to your goal than you are today. If you want to be successful in your life, then practise success. Don't let inexperience or fear of failure prevent you from taking that first step towards your goal. Don't let doubt block your mind.

Take a look at your life. Pick five things that have made you feel small, or helpless, or grumpy, or sad in the last week. Now pick five that have made you feel happy, or clever, or loved, or like you're actually getting somewhere. When I did this every week, very soon I found myself writing down more good things than bad things.

Negative experiences have a habit of growing in our minds and overshadowing the good things. If you change your perspective, niggling little worries will get smaller, allowing you to focus your energy on the positives. These positives don't have to be big world-changing events. Enjoy the small victories in life: watching raindrops run down a window on a rainy day; remembering to take the food out of the freezer for dinner; finally remembering the phone number you've been having to look up for months; managing to get up, dressed, fed, and out of the house with a smile on your face. These are all examples of moments where you have won. If you focus on these moments rather than the ones where it feels like the world is conspiring against you, then you will be well on your way to unblocking your energy.

The power of the written word

Start a personal journal – a reflection of your inner self and your journey to achieving spiritual unity with the Universe, not a daily diary. Choose a format that works for you, whether it is a document on your computer, a note on your tablet or smartphone, a paper notebook, or a collection of papers kept in a folder or ring-binder. It is important that your journey is your own.

Personally, I like to write my journal out longhand, as when I first get an idea, I find that it flows more easily through a pen than through a keyboard. This means I can generate a record of my thoughts quickly and then type it up on the computer later. I also like to keep a notebook on hand where I can record all my thoughts and ideas throughout the day. This is personal to me, and is a great help when I come to write or to reflect.

Write in your journal at the end of each day, exploring your thoughts, feelings, wishes and desires. Each day, you will encounter different difficulties and possibilities, and these experiences will shape your journal. In turn, your journal will shape your future, allowing you to design your perfect life.

Write your story in the past tense, as if it has already happened to you. Avoid writing negative things down – your journal is a place solely for the positive. If you use good, positive words about the life you would like to live and the goals you would like to achieve, you will produce the right vibrations. Remember – what you think becomes what you are and do. This is the Law of Attraction at work.

The power of the spoken word

Once you have begun to design your perfect life by writing your inner thoughts, emotions and desires in your journal, give them more impact by engaging with the power of the spoken word.

Once a week, recite the contents of your journal out loud. By articulating what you want and need, you will be cementing your desires, increasing the efficacy of the Law of Attraction in your life. You will also be boosting your confidence. The more you write down your wishes and read them aloud, the more the Universe will bring them to you.

Meditation

Meditation is the act of entering into a higher level of consciousness. When all the toxic debris is cleared from your cosmic energy channels by your new, positive way of thinking, you will be ready to communicate with the Universe through meditation.

Because you are going to communicate directly with the most powerful force in existence, you need as much help as possible. You will be tapping into the power of the Moon, which has an enormous effect on our planet and tides – and on us. The human body is about

95% water, so the gravitational effects of the Moon have an impact on our mood and physiology. You will also need to call on the help of the four key elements of nature: Water, Fire, Earth and Air.

The metaphysical plane exists on a much higher level of consciousness than the physical plane. To bridge the gap between these two levels of existence, we must use the intrinsic power of our mind. It is impossible to visit the metaphysical plane in a physical form. Instead, develop a spiritual form – only then can your spiritual journey truly begin.

A positive attitude not only provides a more pleasant path by which to move through life, it also increases basic energy levels. Put simply, thinking positively gives us more spiritual power. Our aura – the expression of our spiritual energy – acts like a magnet. When we think positively, we attract good things, and when we think negatively, we attract bad things.

Remain aware of how you approach a situation; keep your thinking and attitude positive and worthwhile. Your emotions play a big part in meditation, so never meditate when you are feeling negative or you will simply amplify your aura's power to attract negativity. Whenever you feel negative thinking creeping into your mind, recognise it and dismiss it immediately. Make the effort to clear your energy channels, detoxify your thinking and purify your mind. Remember, the mind is your gateway to the cosmic forces. Calm down, have a cup of tea, and come back to meditation when you are in a more positive frame of mind.

First and foremost, meditation allows you a space in your possibly hectic life that is entirely your own, even if you only have time for ten minutes. Meditation is a good way of letting go of the stresses of the day, leaving you ready to face the world feeling refreshed, peaceful and strong.

There are many types of meditation and relaxation, so I will share a few basic techniques that have worked for me. You may find that different things will work for you; since meditation is a personal experience, the way we approach it will be equally individual.

Open your mind and let your thoughts flow. When you feel

your consciousness unfold, separating from your body, you will be at peace with yourself. Simply rejoice in this feeling for a moment. I describe this sensation as nirvana – a beautiful place filled with love. There is a tremendous sense of safety between your mind and the Universe. Here, I feel warm, comfortable, loved; like nothing can hurt me at all; as if I am a child in my mother's arms.

At this stage, you are ready to ask the Universe for your heart's desire, though it may be best to practise reaching this level of consciousness a few times before you do so. Even if you have nothing to ask of the Universe, it is worth taking a little time every so often to put your mind into a state of spiritual peace. It sounds corny, but it really is good for the soul.

After analysing all the areas of my spiritual awareness, I found that my weakest area was meditation. I was determined to improve, so I established a habit of meditating for five minutes a day – sometimes twice daily. Before I meditate, I like to do some breathing exercises and stretch my limbs, preferably in the vicinity of an open window. You may have heard it too many times in your childhood, but a bit of fresh air really is good for you.

I am lucky in that I live by the sea, and when the weather is suitable I take a walk on the beach to clear my mind in preparation for my meditation. Since meditation is an individual experience, you will need to find your own ideal place or situation to clear your mind. Often people find peace in natural surroundings, so experiment with taking a short walk through local woodland or parks, perhaps along a river or a canal. Find the places that bring you the most calm.

Some people go through the motions of prayer, hymn singing, confessions, genuflection and so on, even if they no longer hold any beliefs associated with these actions. They are simply behaviours that bring some measure of comfort or peace to them.

Set aside a time for meditation. You may find that you are happier starting the day with meditation, while others prefer to do it when they come in from work or school to de-stress after a long day. Whichever you prefer, find a space in which you feel comfortable, and make sure there are no distractions. Trying to relax in front of an enormous pile of ironing won't work, nor will attempting to meditate surrounded by work notes and reports. Clear the space you are in of pressures and distractions, even if it means putting the ironing in the hall for a few minutes. Meditation must be performed in the right environment, or you will not be able to benefit fully from the experience. Switch off the television, radio and any other electronic devices. Make sure there are no people or pets around to interrupt the calmness of your being. If you have a young family, meditate when they are sleeping or at school, or ask your partner to take care of them for an hour.

Many people find music an aid to meditation, while others find it distracting. This can vary depending on your mood, so don't worry if the instrumental selection that worked for you last week isn't working today – go with the flow. If you choose to listen to music, find something without a strong beat or your subconscious won't be able to relax. A calm, specially selected meditation track can aid your experience, or perhaps another sound will make you feel relaxed – this could be birdsong, it could be silence. Natural sounds are best – there are suitable selections available on YouTube and Spotify. Because I have many years of experience in meditation, I can easily tune in to the harmonies of the Universe without the aid of any sounds at all.

The temperature in the room you choose to meditate in must be just right for you – find a comfortable point. You will be engaging in a period of stillness, so it is important that you don't allow your body to get too cold, but you also don't want to overheat. Wear loose clothing and remove any footwear. Loose clothing allows your body to move, breathe and relax. If you wear supports for joints that you feel you need to keep on, then do so, but this activity is not strenuous, so you may not need them.

Tone down the lighting a little. Recent studies have indicated that we are at our most relaxed in dim or gentle lighting. Our bodies take the fading light as a visual cue to wind down, ready for sleep. A bright light, whether it's the midday sun or a high-powered electric light, will keep your body more on edge and you will be unable to achieve the relaxation required for effective meditation.

I would advise you to avoid food, drink and sex for at least one hour before performing meditation due to the temporary changes in body chemistry that these activities evoke. Similarly, avoid interacting with screens that have a blue light component – these include televisions, computer monitors, tablets, smartphones and the like. Blue light, like bright sunlight, can prevent our brains from relaxing. For the same reason, it is advisable to avoid blue light for at least half an hour before sleeping.

If you are a yoga enthusiast, you will already be aware of the importance of proper breathing and muscular relaxation, but if not, here's a brief crash course.

Breathing

Controlling your breathing can have health benefits outside of meditation, particularly if your life – like many people's – is stressful at times. It can calm you down ready for sleep, or even lower your blood pressure.

Here are a few of the most effective breathing exercises that can be used in a wide range of situations, from preparing for meditation to calming down before an all-important job interview.

Equal breathing, or Sama Vritti. The core idea behind this technique is balance. I think it's safe to say that we could all do with a little more of that in our lives.

Begin by inhaling through your nose, counting steadily to three while you do so, then breathe out in the same way, counting steadily to three. Repeat this up to ten times, depending on how stressed you are currently feeling. The more often you practise this technique, the longer a count you will be able to maintain – sometimes up to eight counts per breath – but aim for staying at around three to five counts per breath for now.

Not only is this technique excellent for increasing focus ready for meditation, it is also great for reducing stress.

Abdominal breathing. This is another technique which is good for relieving stress, and it has been known to help lower blood pressure.

Place one hand lightly on your chest and the other lightly on your stomach. Breathe in deeply and steadily through the nose, making sure that the diaphragm inflates with enough air to create a stretch in the lungs – don't simply fill your lungs with air.

Not sure where to find your diaphragm? It's the hard-working muscle directly below your lungs and the chief culprit for giving you hiccups. You can feel it as a tense wall of muscle a little way below your ribs.

You'll know when you're getting this breathing technique right because both the hand on your belly and the hand on your chest will register movement, not just the one on your chest. Think of it as the difference between your breathing when you chuckle and your breathing when you give a deep belly laugh and you won't go too far wrong.

Build your sessions up to six to ten deep, slow breaths per minute for five minutes a day. Needless to say, if you have a breathing condition, speak to your doctor before attempting this exercise. If you begin to feel light-headed at any point, stop and take it easy for a few minutes and pick it up again tomorrow. If the light-headedness persists, please speak to a medical professional.

Alternate nostril breathing, or Nadi Shodhana. This is a powerful pre-meditation aid, both calming and balancing your mind and body, but don't do it before you want to sleep as it is designed to wake you up and clear your mind. It's also best to avoid this technique if you have a cold, or the consequences could be a little unpleasant.

Get into a comfortable meditative position – you may already have your own preferences, but if not, start out by sitting straight backed and cross-legged on the floor. Hold your right thumb over your right nostril and inhale deeply through the left nostril. Imagine you are inhaling a cold remedy or decongestant, but keep the breath steady. At the peak of inhalation (just before you begin to exhale), place the forefinger of your right hand over your left nostril and remove your thumb from your right nostril. Exhale through your right nostril.

Next, hold the left thumb over your left nostril and inhale deeply through the right nostril. This time, at the peak of inhalation, place the forefinger of your left hand over your right nostril and exhale through your left nostril.

Continue in this pattern a few times.

Basic stretches

You are likely to find a group of stretches that will suit you, but here are a few examples to get you started. Don't worry if you find them difficult – with practice comes ease.

If you find that one of these stretches hurts, stop doing it immediately. That one may not be for you, but have faith – we are all built differently, and you *will* find stretches that work for you. Have a look on the internet or in books in the library for yoga techniques, or speak to a yoga instructor to find out what the best mix of stretches for you to practise may be.

Loosen up. This is a good exercise for loosening stiff muscles. Stand with your feet about a foot apart and wriggle the toes of your left foot. Then lift it slightly from the floor (steady yourself on the wall or the back of a chair if you need to) and make small circles with it from your ankle. Make the circles wider until all of your leg below the knee is involved.

Repeat the process with your right leg.

Next, wriggle the fingers of your left hand, then make small circles with your hand from the wrist, increasing the radius gradually. Keep going until the whole arm is involved.

Repeat the process with your right arm.

Next, shake your hands – imagine you're trying to get water off them. Continue the shaking until it moves up your arms. Wiggle your torso, allowing the movement to pass down your body and into your legs, right down to your feet.

Have fun with it, and relax.

Standing and balancing. This is a good exercise if you are a little out of sorts – it can really help you feel more centred. It's also good for stretching out your back if you've been sitting at a desk all day.

Stand with your feet parallel and a few inches apart. You should feel comfortable and stable, with the soles of your feet flat on the floor. Let your arms hang loosely by your sides.

Begin the stretch in your legs, lengthening them. Raise up and draw in the muscles in your lower abdomen; at the same time, relax your shoulders and buttocks. Stretch the back of your neck upwards, dropping your chin a little.

Maintaining this stretch, reach downwards slightly with your fingers, lengthening the muscles in your hands and arms. Now, keeping your breathing slow and even, focus on a point straight ahead of you – this will help you to maintain your balance while you move through the next stage of the exercise.

As you breathe in, raise your arms upwards until they are above your head, gently bringing your heels off the floor at the same time. Hold this position for a moment, then lower your heels and arms, breathing out gently, and return to a standing position.

Repeat this exercise a few times, keeping your breathing slow and calm. While this may not seem like the most advanced of positions, it does take a little while to maintain and complete the stretch without feeling wobbly, so don't lose heart.

Forward bend. The forward bend is useful if you're feeling stressed, and it can help you to concentrate, especially if you intend to meditate afterwards.

If you suffer from back problems or sciatica, it may be best to avoid this exercise. If in doubt, seek professional advice from a qualified yoga practitioner, or your GP. Always remember, yoga positions should challenge and stretch your body, but they should never hurt – if an exercise hurts, stop doing it.

Stand with your feet parallel and a few inches apart, the soles of your feet flat on the floor. Breathe in slowly and steadily, lifting your arms above your head. As you breathe out, bend forward from your hips. Keep your back long and not curved. Move your arms down as you bend, bringing your hands and fingers to the floor. Stretch your hands so they are palm downwards, flat on the floor.

Don't worry if you can't reach at first – many of us have tightness or stiffness in our backs and legs, often as a result of working at a desk all day. The goal of this exercise is not to be able to touch the floor or your toes, but to unlock your back. As with all exercises, it will become easier the more you practise. If you cannot reach the floor at first, bend your legs at the knee until you feel comfortable in the position. You can also bring your hands to your shins instead of the floor. The more often you complete the exercise, the closer to the floor you will be able to reach.

Your back should feel released and no longer tense in the forward bend. Relax your neck and face, along with your upper back. Inhale, slowly swinging your body upright and bringing your arms back above your head. Breathe out and relax.

Repeat this exercise several times.

Shoulder stretch. This is great for relieving tension in the arms and shoulders, though do avoid this stretch if you have an arm injury or shoulder problems.

Kneel on the floor in a comfortable position – you may find a yoga mat useful here. Keeping your back and neck straight and relaxed, breathe in, lifting your right arm overhead. Bend it at the elbow, reaching down behind you with the palm facing the centre of your back. At the same time, reach your left arm behind you, palm facing outward, and link the fingertips of both hands.

Continue to breathe slowly and steadily. When you breathe out again, stretch your back slightly, tucking the muscles of your abdomen in. Hold this position for several breaths, whatever feels most comfortable for you (three to five is a good amount to aim for), and then bring your arms back to rest on your knees.

Keeping your back and neck straight and relaxed, breathe in and repeat the exercise, this time lifting your left hand overhead and linking it with your right hand behind your back. You may find that you have more difficulty completing this exercise on one side than the other. This is because the dominant arm is often stiffer than the other, and is harder to bring into the lower position.

Head to knee. Take care with this one if you suffer from lower back pain. This exercise stretches the legs, increasing breath control and hip flexibility.

Sit on the floor on a yoga mat so that your back is straight and comfortable, and your neck is relaxed. Stretch your left leg out in front of you and tuck up your right leg so that your foot is resting against your left thigh. Think of it as sitting half cross-legged, if that helps.

Stretch your left leg, drawing your foot upright so that it is perpendicular to the floor. The top of your foot should be pointing towards you. Breathing in, raise your arms above your head, stretching and lengthening your whole body upwards. As you breathe out, bend forward over your outstretched leg. Place your hands palm down on the floor either side of your leg, continuing to breathe slowly and steadily. Stay in this position for three to five breaths (or as long as you can manage).

Straighten out your back, sitting up.

Next, repeat the exercise, this time stretching your right leg out in front of you and tucking your left leg up so that your foot is resting against your right thigh.

Straighten out your back, sit up and relax.

Posture

Posture is one of the key things to master when it comes to meditation. With this in mind, it is worth thinking about your suitable meditation position now. The default position is sitting cross-legged on the floor – if your floor is not carpeted, it is very much worth your while investing in a rug or yoga mat for your meditation, if you don't already have one. There is nothing quite like cramp for ruining your concentration.

It may be that sitting cross-legged on the floor is uncomfortable or impossible for you. Fear not – this doesn't mean you cannot practise meditation. Simply find a position that meets the following criteria:

- You must be still
- You must be able to maintain this position for at least five minutes
- You must be comfortable, but make sure you are not so comfortable that you fall asleep
- Your spine should be straight and well supported by your stomach and back muscles – think about someone telling you to sit up straight, but don't be tempted to tip your head back
- Your neck should be supporting the weight of your head, but not tense – imagine that you have a piece of string attached to the back of your skull and someone is pulling it taut

For most of us, sitting in a chair with a solid, flat seat, high enough for us to place our feet flat on the floor or gently cross our ankles, will be ideal. Avoid meditating lying down, except when you're trying out the beginner's example below. Don't meditate on a sofa; it won't support your body properly, and you may be tempted to slump or fall asleep.

Rest your hands on your thighs and relax the muscles in your face, neck and shoulders, without allowing your head to tip forwards or backwards – and there you have it. You're ready to get started.

Basic meditation techniques

If this is your first attempt at meditation, don't worry whether or not you'll be good at it – this isn't something you can be good or bad at. This fact alone is remarkably liberating.

Start gently. Lie on your back on the floor, preferably on a rug or yoga mat so that your muscles don't get cold. If you have problems lying down, this exercise is perfectly possible on a chair. Find a position that is comfortable for you.

Arrange your limbs in such a way that they are relaxed. Some people find that clasping their hands over their stomach works best; some may find that having their arms at their sides is most comfortable; some may prefer to lie in a starfish shape – whatever works for you.

Close your eyes. Listen.

Listen to the room around you. There may be a clock ticking, or children playing outside. Accept the sound, then forget it.

Listen to your breathing. Listen to each inhale and exhale, and allow the rhythm of your breathing to calm your mind.

Find your heartbeat. Though we spend most of our lives unaware of it, it can always be heard if we listen for it. Feel the blood pulsing through your body with each steady beat.

Focus on your heartbeat and breathing. Don't try to alter them, or worry that the beat is too fast or slow, or that you aren't breathing deeply enough. Accept them for what they are in that moment.

Become aware that your body is relaxing.

Remain like this – quiet, and peaceful, and aware – until you are completely relaxed. Because you are focusing on your breathing and heartbeat, you should be able to push complex thoughts away. Forget what you're having for dinner, or when your report needs to be in. Learn to *be*.

After my experience of absolute peace and oneness on the beach in Miami, I found the feeling became elusive. Although I knew what the feeling represented – a breakthrough into a higher plane of existence – I found it hard to get that moment of powerful knowledge back.

Fortunately, I have now perfected the technique of tapping into that experience. I am able, through diligent practice, to shut off from my conscious surroundings and focus on my subconscious. Through meditation, I can allow my mind and soul to float to a more spiritual level – and so can you. Thinking at this level will bring you closer and closer to the Universe.

Show gratitude

Never take anything for granted.

Thank the Universe. Show gratitude for all that you have and all that you are. You are precious and valuable and incredible. You are wonderful, like the Universe. Give thanks for every little part of you that makes you who you are.

I show my gratitude all the time, thanking the Universe for its great and mighty gifts. Thank you, thank you, thank you – I cannot thank the Universe enough. The inner peace and completeness that it provides had been missing from my life.

Sadly, so many people go through their entire lives without ever discovering this beautiful and rewarding gift. Why would anyone choose to miss out on such a powerful connection with the Universe?

As I graduated through each stage of the process, my subconscious mind became stronger and I was able to speed up my meditative sessions to attain connection with the Universe. As with all things in life, diligent practice and faith in both the process and yourself do eventually pay off. If you ask the Universe to aid you in your journey of spiritual discovery – meeting the Universe halfway – you will be rewarded.

Have a plan

Ask yourself what you want from life. Write out a series of goals and when you'd like to achieve them. It's easy to get carried away here and commit yourself to an impossible timescale, so be realistic with yourself.

The traffic light system is a useful way of prioritising your goals. First write down the ten things that you feel are most important for you to achieve. Your goals will evolve as you evolve, so some will change over time and some will stay the same. The great thing about the traffic light system is that you can easily update it.

Break down your ten goals into three timescales, and colour code the timescales. Green goals are things you want to achieve in the next month, amber goals are those you want to achieve in the next six months, and red goals are the things you want to achieve in the next year. You are likely to find your goals divided evenly, with three in two of the timescales categories and four in the third.

You now have a go-to map of your immediate goals, which will allow you to keep those priorities in mind while you plan how to tackle each goal. The best way to achieve a goal that feels overwhelming is to treat it like a 'whale sandwich'. There is no way you could eat a whole whale in one gulp, so break it down into bite-size pieces.

Here is a common example of a goal that the majority of people will work towards at some point in their lives: learning to drive. Once this goal has been prioritised, next it needs breaking down into bitesize pieces:

- Save up for the cost of a provisional licence, lessons, the written test and the practical test
- Get passport photographs taken
- Organise paperwork to apply for a provisional driving licence
- Get the paperwork checked
- Send the paperwork off
- Research driving schools in your area
- Read up and study for the written test
- Decide on a driving school that works for you
- Once your provisional licence has arrived, book driving lessons
- Attend driving lessons, continue studying for the written test and practise driving in your own time
- Having discussed it with your instructor, book the written test
- Take the written test
- Having discussed it with your instructor, book the practical test
- Take the practical test
- Pass it
- Apply for a full driving licence

With a little luck and a lot of hard work, once you have consumed all your bite-size pieces, you will have completed your goal. Initially, learning to drive is a red goal, but it moves up through amber and green as time progresses and you get closer to realising it. Because you took the time to plan the completion of your goal in detail, you started off with a good idea of the timescale, steps and effort required. Planning is an important step, as it will prevent you from feeling overwhelmed.

Remember, your thoughts become your reality. Think positively, plan effectively and never give up.

Take control of your life

Ready? Set…go!

At this stage, you are likely to be all fired up. You may think that nothing can stop you now, but unless you maintain that enthusiasm on a daily basis, there is a danger of it waning, leaving you struggling to keep up with the goals you have set for yourself. This can be disheartening.

To avoid losing your enthusiasm, persevere. Do as my gran advised me to do all those years ago: take a picture of your goal – be it a car; a slimmer waistline; a house of your own – and stick it on your bedroom wall or bedside table. That way, that image will be the first thing you see in the morning and the last thing you see at night. Your enthusiasm will stay at its peak and you will feel like you can overcome every obstacle. You will be able to meet each challenge that comes your way and change your life for the better.

Remember, *you* are powerful. You *can* do this. You *will* do this. Have a little faith in yourself; you are worth it.

> Our deepest fear is not that we are inadequate. Our deepest fear is that we are powerful beyond measure. It is our light, not our darkness that most frightens us. We ask ourselves, 'Who am I to be brilliant, gorgeous, talented, fabulous?' Actually, who are you not to be?
>
> Marianne Williamson

Signposts

Honesty

With the best will in the world, if you cannot be honest with yourself, you will never find true contentment.

Your life is a journey. Sometimes the map gets a little crumpled; sometimes people will want to lead you away from your path. Do not be pressured into living the way other people want you to live. Some obstacles are unavoidable, but far more frequently we create obstacles for ourselves. Take your life into your own hands and take responsibility for your decisions – once you have done that, you will be ready to let the wonderful things the Universe has in store for you soak in.

When it comes to the big decisions in life, make sure that you are comfortable with the way you are choosing to go. This is why you need a clear idea of the life goals you are aiming for. Remain true to yourself, your beliefs and your journey. Don't let yourself get caught up in what the modern world expects you to be. If you can't be true to yourself, then you can never be open to the gifts and opportunities that are just around the corner.

Here is an example of a time when I had to be honest with myself, no matter how big an upheaval it would cause in my life.

My business was in Suffolk, and at the time I lived in Sussex, over 100 miles away. It was very inconvenient to travel back and forth all the time, so I realised I had to move closer to the hotel in which I worked.

When I had been honest with myself and set myself the goal of selling my house, this is the list I created to help me achieve that goal:

- Contact an estate agent
- Put the house on the market
- Organise viewings and ensure that I was there while they were taking place in order to show the house in the best possible light
- Continue to organise viewings until the house sold
- Find a new property in Suffolk
- Purchase the new property in Suffolk
- Arrange for a removal company to pack and transport my belongings
- Unpack my belongings in my new home – and then the mission would be complete

If you feel lost under the weight of a difficult decision, take some time out. Occupy yourself and take your mind off the decision, then listen to the Universe. If the decision is the wrong one for you, the Universe will let you know. If it is the right one, you will know it, too.

Honesty is always the best policy.

Do your bit

You didn't think that the Law of Attraction fairy would wave her magic wand and instantly grant your heart's desire, did you? I'm afraid it doesn't work like that – the Universe is not a shopping catalogue. Do not expect to visualise the car of your dreams and have it arrive on your drive the next day.

As with all things in life, you need to put time and effort into achieving your goals. You simply won't get anywhere without a bit of old-fashioned elbow grease. Meet the Universe halfway.

If you want that new car, use the Law of Attraction and positive thinking to realise your dream, but also make sure you've passed the relevant driving test and are saving up for it. Want a beautiful garden? Imagine the garden of your dreams in perfect detail, focus on that image every morning when you get up and every night when you go to sleep, and it won't be long before you are relaxing in it – but don't forget to order the seeds, read up on propagation and get ready for some serious digging.

The Law of Attraction isn't about getting things for free; it's about getting what you want and need through hard work and manifestation, helping others, and good planning. The gifts we receive from the Universe wouldn't be half so rewarding if we didn't have to work for them. Sometimes the Universe wants you to feel the singular pride you only encounter when you have done something incredible. The satisfaction of being able to make the most delicious blackberry crumble in the world, for example, would be greatly diminished if you'd never got it wrong and had to feed it to the dog. Relish the journey, take lots of pictures and learn from it.

Giving

Part of our unspoken agreement with the Universe needs to be that we will use our good fortune to make life better for others. Don't be afraid of giving. Give to family members; give to friends; choose a couple of charities you really believe in and give to them.

A gift doesn't have to be monetary, though. You can give your time, labour, patience. Think about times in your life when what you needed most was a friend to have a cup of tea with, and be that friend. Do someone a favour when they're having a hard time of it, or help out an elderly or less able neighbour. Maybe someone you know needs a hand with their gardening, or to build a tree house for their kids, or a little company, or to maintain a community project. Use the skills and experience you have developed over a lifetime to help others become receptive to the Universe, too. It's incredible what getting rid of just one big worry can do for a person.

Remembering my experiences in Liverpool as a young man, I would like to start a charity for people who are down on their luck – the homeless – to help them get back on their feet and regain their independence. The proceeds from the sales of this book will go towards the charity's foundation, and I intend to hold regular workshops too, demonstrating the art of communication with the cosmic forces.

Look for volunteering opportunities in your area. Volunteering, like giving, is a remarkably rewarding experience. Not only are you helping someone (which is a marvellous feeling in itself), but also it may give them the strength to accept their own miracles.

Giving is a reward in itself – but that's not why we do it. We do it because it will make someone else happier, or safer, or more comfortable. The Universe gives us so much, so it's only fair that we pass the favour on.

Karma

Karma is the idea that energy is produced by our deeds – both good energy and bad energy; good karma and bad karma. The principle of karma is fundamental to Buddhism, but it can be applied in almost every set of beliefs. Focus your energy on creating good karma by doing good deeds (you may have heard the American phrase 'paying it forward' – this is more or less the same thing).

The more bad things you do – 'bad' meaning anything that hurts someone, be it others or yourself – the more bad karma you will build up. Bad karma invites negativity, frustration and disaster into your life. If you cannot do right by yourself and others, then the Law of Attraction will not be able to fulfil your goals.

The more good things you do, the more good karma you build up, and the more positivity and success you invite into your life. It is vital to maintain good karma in order to achieve your goals – this is part of meeting the Universe halfway.

The concept of karma is not so alien to modern life. In fact, it is often the subject of popular culture. In the sitcom *My Name Is Earl*, for example, an ex-con suffering from excessive bad karma decides to fix all the bad things he's done and get back some good karma.

I first watched Rhonda Byrne's exploration of the subject of karma in her 2006 film *The Secret*, and I could not wait to put her system into practice in my own life. Much to my disappointment, though, I found it did not produce the result I had desired. I put it to one side, intending to try it again at a later point, but the DVD remained on the shelf, gathering dust. I had good intentions, but procrastination had set in.

I have now identified procrastination as my primary adversary in life. Procrastination should be declared public enemy number one!

My beliefs were still a part of me, so I realised that it was not as simple as Rhonda's system not working properly for me; it was something that *I* wasn't doing. I went back to the drawing board to make some adjustments to the way I looked at life and found that my belief system required some fine-tuning.

"You have to give in order to receive" – how often do we hear or use that phrase? It slides so easily off the tongue that it's a wonder that anyone remembers what it's all about. That's part of the trouble with the modern media: it has a habit of appropriating a phrase or sentiment and over-using it until it becomes a meaningless sound bite. "You have to give in order to receive" has become an automatic response associated with do-gooders, as if kindness and compassion are a sort of disease.

What does it really mean?

Another murdered phrase is "You don't get something for nothing". When you use the Law of Attraction in your life, you are entering into a two-way contract with the Universe. There's no point expecting miracles to work without putting in a little hard graft yourself, and this is as true of karma as it is of any other part of your life. You can no more expect positive things to happen to you if you are neglecting your fellow creatures or the planet you live on than you can drive without first obtaining a licence.

Have you ever heard the phrase, "Do as you would be done by" (meaning treat people the way you want to be treated)? Karma isn't just about what you do; it's about what you think, too. You may believe that your inner thoughts are private, but actually all your thoughts, words and deeds are picked up by the Universe. They are then processed, magnified and returned to you in kind.

If you don't want negativity or spite in your life, then erase negative and spiteful thoughts from your mind. The Universe can't tell the difference between positive and negative thoughts. It will magnify and reflect whatever you are focusing your mind and energy upon, so ensure that you are focusing on the right things. If bad thoughts or feelings enter your mind, recognise them for what they are and dismiss them. Tell them firmly and clearly that they are not welcome – if it helps, find a private space and tell them to be off out loud. This kind of negativity has no place in your life.

Do not seek revenge on people who have wronged you or hold any bitterness towards them. Quite apart from the fact that bitterness is an unhealthy attitude to maintain, the Universe will magnify it and send it back to you. Learn to forgive. By doing this, you are unblocking your energy channels and allowing the flow of vibrations to the Universe.

It is worth remembering that everyone is giving out vibrations all the time, both positive and negative. If you go through life annoying or upsetting people, not only will those people not be especially concerned when you fall on hard times, they will reflect your bad vibrations back at you, magnified by their own negative thoughts of you. Conversely, if you treat others with the respect and friendship they deserve, they will reflect your positivity back to you.

Keep an eye on the kind of karma you're creating and you can't go far wrong.

If you are interested in finding out more about karma and its influence on your life, Rhonda Byrne's 2006 book and film *The Secret* is a great place to start.

Mantra

Don't underestimate the power of mantra. A phrase or sentence that truly represents your goal can keep you on track or spur you on to greater heights.

The word 'mantra' is derived from the Sanskrit for a sacred utterance or group of words. Essentially, it describes the act of giving power to certain words or groups of words through repetition and belief.

The power of the spoken word can be extraordinary when it has been practised to perfection. A phrase or promise designed around your goals and repeated daily will be transferred to your subconscious mind where it can take root and grow, informing your conscious thoughts. This is a powerful means of making changes in your life.

Many people in the modern world feel that their life is not entirely their own. Work, finances and family tensions can make them feel they have lost control over their lives, which can be an enormous emotional burden. The first example of mantra that I want to share can be used to help you feel more in control. It can also establish and reinforce an atmosphere of positive thought and good karma in your life.

Repeat the following phrases:

- I am in full control of my thinking
- I will only let good thoughts enter my head
- I will only think good of others
- I will only speak the truth

Establish a habit of repeating this and any other mantra of your choice five times a day, but don't worry if this seems like a lot at first. If it feels too daunting, start off with once a day just before you get up and build up from there. Before long, you will find yourself repeating your mantra – and really meaning it – five times a day. It will become a part of you, changing your attitudes, informing your actions, and reinforcing your beliefs.

The best mantras are well-thought-out, meaningful phrases,

but you don't have to be a poet in order to benefit from them. Pick a phrase that is positive in nature and, more importantly, means something to you. If it doesn't mean a thing to you, then it won't work.

Your mantra may be something as simple as, "Today, I will find three things to smile about", or as complex as the translation of the Gayatri mantra, "Let us meditate on that excellent glory of the divine Light. May he stimulate our understandings", which is often considered to be the most universal of the Hindu mantras. There are thousands of mantras available to choose from – a quick search on the internet will provide a long list of options. Use quotations, poetry, song lyrics – even a positive internet meme can work as a mantra if it speaks to you. Just make sure that you know what it means to you, and do not simply repeat the mantra, automatically going through the motions each time. This will get you nowhere. Really believe in the words. A mantra is an inherently personal thing, so it must reflect the impact you want it to have in your life.

A common burden shared by many people across the world is ill health, so the second mantra I wish to share with you is designed to help restore and maintain good health. This mantra also allows you to give thanks to the Universe at the same time as tapping into its awesome power:

> Oh mighty Universe,
> Hear my voice.
> Please help me,
> Please restore my health.
> I am truly grateful to you,
> I love you.
> Thank you for everything you have given me.

As with all things in life, if you put the effort into finding and repeating your mantras, you will reap the rewards. A mantra is like a promise you make to yourself and the Universe. There's no point making a promise if you have no intention of keeping it.

Visualisation

If you do not fully appreciate what it is you want, how can you expect the Universe to arrange for it to happen to you?

If you know you want to save up for a car, choose exactly *which* car. If you're working towards buying your first home, find images of the location and the kind of house you want to live in. Keep these images in mind and you are one step closer to being able to manifest your dreams.

In our daily lives, visualisation makes a deep impression on the subconscious mind. Proper practice will bring you ever closer to the Universe and the forces of nature. Although words have tremendous power, they have no place in visualisation. Words are best placed to aid you as part of a mantra. Visualisation focuses on an image of your goal.

Obviously, some of the things you want will be more abstract concepts than tangible things that you can take a photograph of. If you want to achieve perfection in a particular discipline, for example, think of an image that represents that goal to you. It may be a picture of a stethoscope if you want to excel in medicine, or a chef's hat if you're a cook, and so on.

This representative image is especially important when it comes to looking for a soulmate. Avoid using a photograph of your 'ideal' person; it may well turn out that the person who most closely matches this image is not right for you at all, and in visualising their picture, you are bringing negativity into your life. Instead, visualise something that symbolises the type of relationship you want to have. For example, you may choose an image of intertwined hands, or a pair of wedding bands, or even an old style 'LOVE' tattoo. The symbols of love and happiness are as personal to each individual as the feelings themselves, so find the picture that sums them up for you.

Once you have your picture, the next step is to fix it firmly in your head. Take a copy of the image and stick it up on your wall – somewhere you will see it first thing in the morning and last thing at night. Find the place where that image has the most impact on you and establish a habit of looking at it in a certain way at regular intervals. Take care not to glance at the image and move on. This is the thing you are working towards, the thing that you really want, so take your time and look at it. Memorise every line and shadow of the image until you can see it with your eyes closed.

Unlocking the potential of visualisation

Now the image is ingrained in your memory, unlock the potential of visualisation through meditation.

During your meditation session, conjure up the image of your goal or desire in your mind's eye and concentrate upon it. Look at every facet of shade and colour; focus on what the image is and what it means to you. When you are in the higher state of consciousness brought about by meditation, visualising what it is that you want will act like sending a letter directly to the Universe. You will be telling the Universe exactly what it needs to do to help you out.

The more you practise visualisation, the nearer to perfection you will get. A lot of people become frustrated and give up at the first hurdle; others become disillusioned if their wish is not granted immediately. Do not be one of these people; do not give up and lose hope. If nothing changes straight away, it doesn't mean that visualisation is not working. Sometimes the Universe needs a little time to arrange things – and it knows a good deal better than we do whether we are ready to achieve a particular goal.

For example, wouldn't it be awful if the Universe allowed us to meet our soulmate before we were ready to accept and embrace one another and we missed our chance to be together? Be patient. Who knows what the next step or stage in your life will bring? Sometimes a journey, whether physical, spiritual or intellectual, takes you to places you never expected to find yourself. This is the Law of Attraction at work, bringing you to where you need to be.

To visualise your goals with passion is to manifest them in reality. Change your inner thoughts and images before you attempt to change what's on the outside and the reality surrounding you. If you have faith in yourself and are at peace with your own decisions, past and present, you will achieve what you want in life – and be happy doing it.

> He who controls others may be powerful, but he who has mastered himself is mightier still.
>
> Lao-Tze, Taoist philosopher

Once you have established an image of what you want and how you want to be, your subconscious thoughts will carry you forward. Filter out the bad thoughts and ignore your fears of rejection or failure. Choose to become the person you want to be.

> Oh how we forget
> That everything is a choice
> And we can decide.
>
> Tyler Knott Gregson

Opportunity

Why do some people seem to get all the opportunities in life while others don't get any?

We are all faced with many opportunities and choices. An opportunity can simply be a matter of being in the right place at the right time, or rather, being presented with the circumstances to make that presence (and presence of mind) possible. The important thing to keep in mind about opportunity is that everyone gets the same amount. It may seem that other people get all the chances they need in life, but this is simply not true.

The other half of every opportunity is choice. In our hectic modern lives, it is easy to focus too minutely on the details of living, when simply stepping back and taking a second look at a situation may resolve it for us. Many opportunities come disguised as problems, and often appear at a time in our lives when we are undergoing some trauma or turmoil. The influence of these outside pressures can make it impossible to see an opportunity for what it really is.

Sometimes, even if we have seen a chance for what it is and acknowledged its presence in our lives, we choose not to take advantage of it for fear of failure. Our fear of failure is rooted in healthy self-preservation – this is the mechanism that kicks in when we are faced with a potentially dangerous or harmful situation. We are hardwired to strive for survival, acknowledge danger and take more care because of that knowledge, but in some cases, this evolutionary programming overrides our impulse to move forwards in our lives.

Ironically, when we do not take advantage of the opportunities the Universe is providing for us due to fear of failing, we are guaranteeing that we will fail. Failure is hard and often horrible, but if we never take a step forward that frightens us, we will never fully develop our true potential. We will never achieve closeness with the forces of nature. We will never really be *us*.

Check your belief system and re-evaluate the negative thoughts and influences that are telling you that you can only fail. You will find that these voices, both internal and external, are almost entirely wrong.

Opportunities come in many different guises, so it is important that you sit down and think about the things that happen in your life from time to time. Perhaps there are opportunities already in place, just waiting for you to notice and accept them. Almost any negative situation can be turned into a positive opportunity with the right kind of attitude.

You attract opportunities when you send out a clear message to the Universe about what you want in life and who you want to be. This can be achieved through positive thinking, cosmic ordering, visualisation, mantra, meditation – the list goes on. Whichever path you choose, though, you must meet the Universe halfway. When you come across an opportunity, take it with both hands and run with it for all you are worth. Unless you fully commit your energy to an opportunity, you are depending upon the Universe to provide all the answers. This is not a healthy way of thinking.

Some opportunities are not right for you at a certain time, so be sure to think carefully about any opportunity you come across. What will its impact be on your daily life? Will taking this opportunity have any negative repercussions? As long as you take care to assess each situation fully, you can't go far wrong. Let go of your fears and allow your spirit to soar.

Positivity

Tap into the cosmic forces of power that are all around every one of us. This will be a life-changing experience – it was certainly one that I wished I had discovered earlier in life as it had an enormous impact on my world.

By following the guidelines in this book, you will become a better person, secure in the knowledge that the errors of your past life can no longer affect you, and you will not repeat them in the future. You will become a happier person. Most of the things that we do in life are geared towards the pursuit of happiness – happiness is the emotion that everyone strives for, but few of us (it seems) ever achieve it. You will wake up each day to the life which you have designed, tailored for yourself, and – most importantly – which *you* have made happen.

Your brain is both a transmitter and a receiver – rather like a radio. By 'tuning in' to the correct frequency or vibration of thought, you can communicate with the Universe. If you ensure that you are sending out positive vibrations, positive vibrations are what you will get back, magnified. You will be tapping into the cosmic energy of a power much greater than yourself – think of the impact that could have on your circumstances.

Remember, whatever your present situation is, you have the power to change it. Get ready to change your life for ever.

Belief

I can't express how important belief is.

Your beliefs must be clear and unsullied by negativity and the pressures of modern living. They will keep you strong when times are tough and lift you up when life is at its best. Belief allows all nature's energy to flow in your direction. Granted, it is hard to believe in something that you cannot see, but life is not black and white. It is a journey through a cornucopia of colours – a journey of discovery.

Just because you can't see something doesn't mean that it doesn't exist. Trust that old tenet of archaeology: absence of evidence is not evidence of absence.

Do not allow doubt to creep into your mind. Doubt can crush your chances of success as surely as doing nothing will. If you believe in your heart that you haven't a chance, then you *will* fail. If, however, you allow yourself to believe that you will succeed, then you will eventually, against all odds, succeed.

Scepticism

Your life is a manifestation of the thoughts going on in your head.

Sceptics are inclined to question accepted ideas. They require physical and often absolute proof of a phenomenon in order to accept it. To assess the world around them, they depend on what is known as 'critical thought' – a system of testing and re-testing every sensation, idea or conversation they encounter. This makes them inherently out of tune with the Universe.

Beware of listening to sceptics as they are likely to plant doubt into your mind. This can undermine or destroy your faith and belief in the system and the Universe. Close your mind to all negative suggestions – anyone who pushes you to question the system is pushing you away from the truth.

Sceptics are often losers in life. They won't let the Universe guide them to their perfect lives so they don't recognise opportunities and can never achieve their dreams. Scepticism breeds fear – sceptics want you to be afraid with them.

Also be wary of blind faith. You can believe in the power of the Universe and the Law of Attraction because you will be able to see it in action in your own life.

Depression

It's possible that you have picked up this book because you are at a low point in your life. The first thing I have to say is this: you are not alone. You are not weird, and you are not going to be stuck there for ever. The advice in this book is just that: advice. It may not be right for you, right now, so I would recommend that you seek medical or professional help if you feel that you need it. You are going to be okay, even if you feel at the moment like you aren't.

It is possible to use the Law of Attraction to help you climb out of the darkness, but it's not a quick or easy fix. Let go of the things you cannot change, set out your goals, foster a more positive attitude and plan well, and you will have made a good start.

Courage

Human nature prompts us to lie, both to others and to ourselves, out of fear. Have courage and face your fears head on – you are likely to be astonished at the effect this will have on your inner self. Courage builds confidence and faith in your own abilities, and this confidence will spread out into other areas of your life.

Truth is an incredibly powerful thing. Only ever speak the truth – don't exaggerate; don't embellish; don't try to impress people with 'little white lies'. Be honest with yourself; never hide behind lies or excuses. Lies block your energy channels. Dishonesty will turn you away from the power of the Universe, making you weaker.

Most people go through life without ever discovering the power within them. This is metaphysics, not religion, or astrology, and certainly not mumbo jumbo. The metaphysical mind is where the link between our inner mind and the Universe exists. It is currently beyond our comprehension, though there may be a day when we come to a better understanding of it. Much of our mind has yet to be tapped – whether consciously or unconsciously.

Love and relationships

When you ask the Universe for help in achieving your goals, do not be greedy or grasping. Ask for what you need and no more – don't abuse the system. Respect it, and this respect must extend to others, too.

It is unwise to ask the Universe to intervene where it comes to relationships. While asking for a steady, fulfilling long-term relationship with mutual respect and lots of laughter is perfectly acceptable, asking for a particular person to fall in love with you is not. Not only would that mean asking the Universe to interfere with the free will of another human, it's not healthy for anyone to focus their energy on another person so completely. This can lead to obsession.

It's perfectly natural to fall in love with someone who doesn't feel the same – I'm sure many of us have done it at some point in our lives, and of course, we want them to love us in the same way. What is unacceptable is using any means to force them to love us. Real love, when it happens, happens entirely of its own accord.

Never ask the Universe to hurt someone or to help you get revenge. You will only end up harming yourself. Remember that the Universe is not a fool, but a force for good. If you are asking for something that will hurt someone else – even inadvertently (e.g. "I want to get the manager's position instead of Judy") – then it will simply frustrate your efforts. Things gained with poor intentions come back to haunt us.

When you are asking for help, don't just go through the motions; do it with feeling. You will know when you are connected to the Universe; you will feel it deep in your soul. This is a two-way relationship, so uphold your end of the bargain.

Light a candle

Let's bring this chapter to a close with a powerful practical step you can take to strengthen your relationship with the Universe.

Between you and the cosmos there is a cavernous void. Lighting a candle can help you bridge that void – never underestimate the potential of something as simple as an ordinary candle. Do you remember making a wish before you blew out the candles on your birthday cake as a child? Somehow, almost instinctively, we knew how to stay in tune with the Universe when we were small. In effect, we were sending our conscious thoughts through the power of the candle flame, Fire being one of the basic forces of the Universe. Increase the potential success of any communication in this way, turning a whispered request into a message that is loud and clear.

Establish in your mind exactly what it is that you want before you light your candle. This desire will strengthen your beliefs and bring you one step closer to meaningful communication with the Universe.

I do not pretend to be an expert on the ancient art of candle burning, so for a more complete guide, I urge you to research this concept on the internet or in your local library. However, there follows a brief guide.

One of the most common wishes in anybody's life is to attract wealth – not necessarily to be fabulously, ridiculously rich, but to obtain a certain amount to enable us to purchase a car or a home – so I will focus on finance in this example.

Colour is a complex set of variables to work into meditation. Every colour reflects an individual spiritual vibration. It is important to know which colour matches which vibration and to avoid using the wrong colour for a wish. If you were to use the wrong colour, you would be sending out a conflicting message to the Universe, which may do more harm than good.

If in doubt, use a white candle for your ritual.

The next step is to establish the best time to perform your ritual, and for this you need to turn to astronomy. Each planet represents a certain colour and a certain day (you can find more information on this subject under any decent Candle Magic title), and to attract money you need the help of Venus, which is represented by the colour green and is most powerful on a Friday.

The most influential celestial body of all is the Moon. She controls the wind and tides, and has an enormous effect on our planet and our bodies. Even as small as a human body is compared to the Moon, we are under the influence of her gravity. The best time to perform your candle burning ritual is between a New Moon and a Full Moon. You want to take advantage of the Moon waxing to increase your funds.

Now decide on a mantra (or spell, if you prefer). For example:

Oh mighty Universe,

Hear my plea.
Let money flow my way.
Thank you,
I love you.

There are many mantras to choose from in books or on the internet, or you may wish to compose one of your own to make it more individual.

Close your eyes and imagine a bright green light coming nearer to you, representing your approaching wealth. After two minutes or so, open your eyes and repeat your chosen mantra six times, feeling each word with sincerity. Now go through your meditation process for about twenty minutes, allowing your subconscious to reinforce your request to the Universe.

When you have finished, leave the area in which you performed your ritual, *leaving the candle burning*. Never interrupt the process by blowing out the candle, as this will disturb the spiritual vibration. If you have to extinguish the candle, use a candle-snuffer.

It is vital to ensure that the candle can burn itself out without being disturbed or posing a risk to you or your home. You may find a sturdy metal tray useful, or you may wish to consider purchasing a small candle for this purpose. *Never* leave a lighted candle unattended unless it is secure in a safe area.

Once you have worked through the relaxation, communication and unblocking techniques contained in this book, your old beliefs will clear from your subconscious mind. You will then able to open your mind to a new beginning.

Congratulations! It takes a lot of commitment to get this far.

My Journey

Experience and hope

Throughout our lives, we suffer all kinds of disasters and crises, from the breakdown of relationships, divorce, the loss of a loved one, to bankruptcy, ill health and death. These are enormous, disruptive, horrible events that have a negative impact on our lives, and it is perhaps not surprising that they sometimes push us to lose faith in and re-examine our beliefs.

This is exactly what happened to me. As my beliefs were shattered by the life-changing things I was going through, the negative rubbish broadcast by an insensitive, indoctrinated and greedy media flooded my conscious mind and filtered through into my subconscious mind.

I had lost faith in myself.

Before this, when miracles happened to me, my subconscious

mind was tuned in to the Universe. Even though I wasn't at that time consciously aware of it, I was open to the wonderful opportunities that the Universe had in store for me. However, the shift in my beliefs that occurred after the dark days altered the tuning of my subconscious mind. It was as if I was a broken radio that could only receive one station – I was picking up interference from the negative media and influences surrounding me, trapped in a vicious circle of failure and despair. Believing I could never succeed, I stopped being able to succeed. It became a self-fulfilling prophecy.

Our subconscious mind is working all the time, even when we are sleeping. This is part of the reason we dream. My dreams at this dark time, like my waking hours, were full of negativity. To move on and retune my mind, I needed to rid myself of all this negativity.

I listed all of my negative thoughts on paper in large, bold letters. I cut them out, separating each negative thought from the next, then brought them to life using colour, putting all the energy that leached out of me when negativity took over into embellishing them. This list was now the embodiment of my negative thoughts.

Using my senses of sight, touch, smell and hearing, I burned my negative thoughts one by one, each time speaking aloud the words, "I remove this negative belief from my unconscious mind – it is destroyed in this fire, never to return." This is one of the most powerful unblocking techniques you can use.

It was an enormously liberating experience. The weight of the negativity I had been carrying around with me for years evaporated as the paper burned. I had nurtured my unconscious mind, preparing it for the future, and I was free to fill my life with positivity and inspiration, ready to flourish as I took the next steps in my spiritual journey. This inspiration has matured over many years, which is how I have come to be writing this book.

The subconscious mind

Human beings are capable of around 60,000 thoughts a day, and most of these are subconscious. Our conscious minds are very much the tip of the iceberg in terms of the scope and potential of our brains. All sorts of thoughts filter through our minds, every second of every day.

Dexter Roger Emrit, author of *Awakening the Spirit: You Can* (2009), suggests that when we engage in the act of thinking, we are asking our subconscious mind to generate an answer based on all the information it has ever encountered and its ability to extrapolate abstract outcomes through experience and imagination. For example, have you ever seen a face that you are convinced you know, but cannot put a name to? How many times has that name come to you later, when you aren't consciously thinking about it any more? This is your subconscious at work.

In terms of the Law of Attraction, the subconscious mind is a powerful tool in that it helps us translate our thoughts into our goals. By letting go of my negativity and planting the seed of inspiration, I had begun the process of changing my belief system.

I have now chosen to lead a more solitary life, only letting a few trustworthy friends and family into my inner circle, which gives me more time to concentrate on the more spiritual side of life. This doesn't mean that I have become a self-styled modern-day hermit – far from it. Instead, I have become aware of the damage that idle gossip and the wrong kind of people (those who insist on living their lives in a cloud of negativity) can cause to both my psyche and my emotional well-being.

Without a healthy atmosphere to interact within, we can never hope to stay connected to the vibrations of the Universe. We should endeavour never to upset anyone else, and if we are doing so, it's a good idea to remedy this. Experience has taught me that the jealousy of others – towards myself and my success – was the cause of my downfall. Because others were jealous of me, they were sending out negative thoughts connected to me and my circumstances, which were magnified and reflected back on to my life.

Everyone is sending out vibrations all the time, both good and bad, so take care to surround yourself with positive people you can trust implicitly. I'm not suggesting that you should become a recluse, nor am I suggesting that you should never put yourself in a position where you will meet new people (something I had to do all the time in the hospitality industry), but you may need to re-evaluate whom you spend your time with. If other people are sending bad vibrations your way, they have no place in your life. I appreciate this is trickier than it sounds – remember the agonies I put myself through when I had to part company with Martin? – but if you are brave and face up to the fact that some people no longer fit in with your life, you are ultimately setting yourself up for the happiness and success that only comes from a healthy relationship with the Universe.

One more miracle

When I ran into Tony, I hadn't seen him in eighteen years.

Tony and I had been good friends when we were younger, but we had – as so many friends do over the years – simply drifted apart as our lives took us in different directions. Still, I was glad to see him again.

During our conversation, Tony told me that he was undergoing treatment for cancer. As we talked about his symptoms, they began to sound horribly familiar to me. Realising that I had a lot of the same indicators, I made an appointment to see my doctor, who listened thoughtfully to my concerns and referred me to the hospital for further checks.

One MRI scan, a biopsy, and a plethora of other tests later, I was diagnosed with cancer.

Just hearing the word shocked me to my core. Cancer. Six little letters that changed my entire world. It was something I read about in the paper, something that I was horrified to hear a close friend or relative had, but it was always one step removed from my own body. It was strange, but the thought that it could be happening to *me* was so utterly alien that I existed in a state of numb disbelief for days.

I had been given a death sentence. This was it. I was a goner.

Eventually, I had to accept my fate. My dear wife Lucy and my four children rallied round me. They were incredibly supportive, and I feel very blessed to have such kind and caring people in my life. Lucy came along to all my hospital appointments with me, even for the daily treatments. She was my own personal rock, anchoring me to life.

I needed it.

My mind was all over the place – I just couldn't get my head around the fact that I was dying. D-y-i-n-g. It is a word that had meant little to me until it referred to my own body.

I decided to get my affairs in order, spend as much of the little time I had left with my family as I could, then make a graceful exit. It was during this time that my daughter, Clementine, asked me if there was one thing I really wanted to do – almost like a last wish. I told her that I would dearly love to write a book. I had often thought about writing. It had been on my mind for a while, building up in intensity, but everyday life required so much attention that I had never got around to it. Now, though, the Universe had presented me with the impetus I needed.

Sometimes, when we admit things to others, they become little promises to ourselves. I had told Clementine that I was going to write a book, and nothing was going to get in my way from that point on. I had given myself permission to succeed – and the Universe had listened.

With Clementine's support and encouragement, I made a start. I put pen to paper and the words flowed out of me – then they poured. I couldn't stop. It was as if my subconscious had waited so many years for the opportunity to share what I had experienced and learned, it now wanted to be heard.

The strangest thing was that the book I had intended to write had altered somewhere along the way – now I was writing what I truly wanted to share. The inspiration was there and would not let me sleep. Every time I tried, my head filled up with words and ideas until I had to get up and let it all overflow on to the page.

The manuscript grew and expanded into the very book you are reading right now, but I would never have started it without my daughter – or the cancer.

The cancer treatment was gruelling, as you may expect. Every time I was put in the machine, or felt like giving up, I would repeat my mantra over and over again, keeping the words at the forefront of my mind and allowing them to manifest into reality:

> Oh mighty Universe,
> Please hear me.
> Please help me,
> Please restore my health.
> I am truly grateful to you.
> Thank you.
> I love you.

When the treatment was finally over, my doctor called me in to see him. The cancer, which had been gnawing at my body for months, had gone. I was given the all clear.

This is the greatest gift I have ever been given by the Law of Attraction. I give thanks for this every day.

Conclusion

Sometimes, the act of achieving a goal is a kind of code that allows you a link to the Universe – a direct phone line, complete with dialling code and extension number. The pages of this book and the information contained within them are all the ingredients you need for a full and fulfilling spiritual life – your passport to the Universe.

I would ask you now to arm yourself with a copy of *The Secret*, be it the book (which is excellent) or the DVD, and use it alongside my guidelines to achieve spiritual awareness and a well-rounded life. Together, these two methods – Rhonda Byrne's and my own – will allow you to move forward in your own life. *The Secret* will show you the next step.

These processes and techniques have worked for me – and are *still* working for me. They have changed my life for the better, for ever. I now have absolute belief, making my faith and the power of my subconscious unbreakably strong. I live a life entirely free of doubt. And if they can work for me, they can work for anybody. They can work for you.

I am so grateful to the Universe for this beautiful gift. Because of it, I am a different person, a better person.

Right now, the information you have read in the pages of this book is valuable. If you choose to act upon it and put it into practice, it will become *priceless*. However, if you choose to do nothing with the information, it renders it *worthless*. Which kind of information would you rather have?

In the end, the Law of Attraction does exactly what it says. You attract whatever you think, say, or do.

Lightning Source UK Ltd.
Milton Keynes UK
UKHW040645291118
333105UK00001B/8/P